ON THE SOVEREIGNTY
OF MOTHERS

ON THE SOVEREIGNTY
OF MOTHERS

The Political as Maternal

GIL ANIDJAR

Columbia University Press

New York

Columbia University Press
Publishers Since 1893
New York   Chichester, West Sussex

Library of Congress Cataloging-in-Publication Data
Names: Anidjar, Gil, author.
Title: On the sovereignty of mothers : the political as maternal /
Gil Anidjar.
Description: New York : Columbia University Press, [2024] |
Includes bibliographical references and index.
Identifiers: LCCN 2024011765 (print) | LCCN 2024011766 (ebook) |
ISBN 9780231216432 (hardback) | ISBN 9780231216449
(trade paperback) | ISBN 9780231561280 (ebook)
Subjects: LCSH: Motherhood—Religious aspects. |
Mothers—Religious life. | Feminism—Religious aspects.
Classification: LCC HQ759 .A537 2024 (print) | LCC HQ759 (ebook) |
DDC 155.6/463—dc23/eng/20240514

Cover design: Julia Kushnirsky

para mamá

Narrated Abu Huraira:
A man came to Allah's Messenger (ﷺ) and said, "O Allah's Messenger (ﷺ)! Who is more entitled to be treated with the best companionship by me?" The Prophet (ﷺ) said, "Your mother." The man said, "Who is next?" The Prophet said, "Your mother." The man further said, "Who is next?" The Prophet (ﷺ) said, "Your mother." The man asked for the fourth time, "Who is next?" The Prophet (ﷺ) said, "Your father."

— Sahīh Al-Bukhāri, *Kitāb al-Adab*, 5971

Listen, then. There are, as it were, two mothers of regimes. It would be correct for someone to say that the others spring from these, and correct to call one monarchy and the other democracy, and to say that the Persian type is the full development of the former, while my people's country is the full development of the latter. Almost all other regimes, as I said, are woven from these. Both of them should and must necessarily be present if there is to be freedom and friendship, together with prudence: this is what the argument wishes to set before us when it says that no city will ever have a fine political life if it lacks a share in either of these.

— Plato, *The Laws* 693d

Il y avait chez nous pas mal de mères qui venaient une ou deux fois par semaine mais c'était toujours pour les autres.

— Émile Ajar, *La vie devant soi*

CONTENTS

PREFACE

MOTHERS AND TIME

I am my mother's child. Like every soul on earth, to be more precise, and for countless ages and lifetimes since the beginning of time, I have been mothered. *Over time*, then.

I am my mother's child. I have been mothered. Over time. I claim no singularity thereby, quite the opposite, for I am, in this specific way, in that necessary and undeniable way, *universal*. The universal in me, the universal in us, which is not the equal in us (which might very well be the *unequal* in us), is that we have been mothered. More or less well. More or less *by our own mothers*. Unequal then, perhaps because, though human beings may be *born* equal, everywhere *mothers* are in chains.[1] All mothers? By what chains? Unless we "look at men as if they had just emerged from the earth like mushrooms and grown up without any obligation to each other," as if they were born and grown up without mothers and without mothering.[2] And yet that unequal universal is that we have all been mothered. Over time, I said. Since when and for how long? *Mais il faut vous dire que j'ai jamais su où ça commence et où ça finit parce qu'à mon avis ça ne fait que continuer.*[3]

You would think that this—our being mothered in time and over time—gave us some kind of incentive or insight, a few listening habits, elements of a wisdom worth acquiring or mulling over (like the earth, wisdom has long been figured as a mother), something that merits laboring and elaborating in turn. You would think this would have made us *motherwise.* Have we not learned about teachers from their students? About doctors from their patients? About merchants from their customers? About sovereigns from their subjects? Have we not learned about masters from their slaves, about slaves, from their masters? About witches, even, from their accusers and inquisitors?

Have we not *learned to learn* from our mothers? Like everyone else, I have learned everything, learned to learn everything—more or less well—from being mothered. Like Luisa Muraro, "I tend to think that everything I have learned well was somehow taught to me by my mother herself."[4] Everything? From my mother only? The truth is obviously more and less than that. There were others, of course, there were *other mothers.* There were grandmothers and stepmothers, nurses, aunts, or sisters. And yes, there were fathers sometimes ("nursing fathers" as King James renders the phrase, but other kinds too).[5] There were even brothers. There were healers, teachers and caretakers, guides—there were rabbis—and neighbors and friends and more. There were perhaps servants. There was God too, and there were *other* gods, gods and goddesses, *djinns,* spirits and ghosts, animal spirits and other animal beings. There was land and sea (*terre et mer*, you had to hear it to believe it). There was, you could say, a village. When it comes to mothers and to mothering, further specifics— the sharing, the denials, and yes, the neglect, the violence and worse—have certainly varied from time to place, from gender to class, to culture and polity. But the particular energetic dependence, the enduring openness, the indelible and sedimented imprints (the *maternal writing*), that, immemorial and therefore everlasting, have conditioned and defined us in terms of touch and nourishment, stimulation and frustration, sense and sensibility, speech and gait, clothing and habit (and habituation), presence and absence—to ourselves and to others—socialization and validation, could not have occurred, perdured, or changed without our having been mothered.

Turn each of these into their most negative version if you can face it, as many have or have had to, as many lived or survived— *or did not*. Turn presence into absence or love into hatred, turn sex into death (the womb into a tomb, milk into poison), or turn peace into a desert, sovereignty into slavery. Picture this instead as a virgin birth that, *pietà* that she is, never fails to hold and thus renders every mother culpable.[6] Or imagine an orphanage, a graveyard, a plantation. Turn mothering into *unmothering*.[7] It will still incalculably compute that knotted noun or verb—mother— without which *no collective* and no individual either, no relationality, can be imagined, let alone lived and learned, nor even destroyed.[8] We have all been mothered.

I am my mother's child. You could read this book, therefore, as a personal statement, a personal judgment, an individual instance of a teacher's evaluation. Yes. No. Good. Bad. Good breast, bad breast. That story is more than familiar. And I know (believe me, I know) that such evaluations, such judgments, are most likely to speak of the students themselves (gender and race, class and religion, attention and distraction). There is no reason to contest that it might be so here as well. Today, perhaps more unavoidably than ever, for reasons that include, but are far from exhausted by, gender issues ("what does it matter who is speaking," Samuel Beckett asked within living memory, echoed by Michel Foucault, famous for his laughter, which must be resonating somewhere). In some cases, though, a group of students, perhaps even children (inquisitive children, at times even inquisitors), will come together, as it were. They will have learned and revealed something else, shown some insight and managed to grasp—perhaps, to catch or indeed betray—something, something that tells us about mothers, about their mothers and othermothers. This is a book about mothers.

Iris Murdoch, who had surprisingly little to say about sovereignty in *The Sovereignty of Good*, and only slightly more about mothers, nevertheless evoked, quite suggestively, "an occasion for 'unselfing.'"[9] At least I think this is what Murdoch meant when she wrote that she was offering her

> descriptions in ordinary public words whose meaning is subject to ordinary public rules. Inner words "mean" in the same way as outer words; and I can only "know" my imagery because I know the public things which it is "of," Public concepts are in this obvious sense sovereign over private objects; I can only "identify" the inner, even for my own benefit, via my knowledge of the outer.[10]

Whether this book succeeds at *unselfing*, whether it succeeds at describing mothers and mothering in ordinary public words (a tough act, I confess, being my mother's child), what should come through is in any case less about my own judgment or position-ality (my *personality*, John Bowlby might say), less about private objects, private subjects. It is rather, as Murdoch explains, about outer words, about the public things that "mothers" are of; the public, indeed *sovereign*, beings mothers are. Public words and public things, then, *to, for, and from*—mothers. Words listened to, words about learning and about living, about mothering, with and from mothers. My own as well, obviously. *On the Sovereignty of Mothers* seeks to take the immeasurable measure—I do not say the good or the bad—of mothering, of our having been mothered, our being mothered still.[11]

I am my mother's child, yes, but, I am no Roland Barthes (who "rediscovered" his mother in a photograph that "collected all the possible predicates from which my mother's being was consti-tuted," or in a mourning diary) and no Romain Gary either (and no Émile Ajar, though that is a different story).[12] I do not feel par-ticularly close to Saint Augustine, that more famous North Afri-can mother-lover whom Jacques Derrida liked so much (JD too took, if more subtly, after his mother, or mothers).[13] Even Jesus's contribution remains strange to me, who asked his disciples to hate their mother (and, admittedly, other family members). This is not Jesus's most celebrated side, I'll grant, but it seems to me his enduring legacy, one we have moreover adopted as a model of emancipation, political and otherwise, as a model of freedom. While Mary was languishing outside, did Jesus not ask, "Who is my mother?" and proceed to ignore her? To be fair, Jesus was pointing, no less remarkably, to a few other mothers instead.[14] For my part, I neither wished to contribute to nor tried to write this or another "mother and son" story. I would not sing "Mother,"[15] nor make a movie by that title,[16] to say nothing of narrating the "mother / daughter plot," which, rarer, no doubt, and perhaps stranger too, has surely been done better than I could (Elena Ferrante!).[17]

And since I have referred to likely (or rather, unlikely) predecessors, I might also mention that René Descartes never subjected his mother (as opposed to his body, his dreams, or his madness) to doubt, to philosophical doubt, leaving it to readers to decide whether, poorly remembered as she may have been (she died in childbirth when René was but a toddler left in the care of his grandmother), she was spared doubt's world-ending (or reputation-ending) consequences, whether she posthumously survived it, much as common wisdom has it (it is, after all, the father who is in doubt, *not* the mother, or so we are repeatedly told). One might be moved to surmise that Descartes, *bereft of a clear and distinct idea of motherhood*, owed Jeanne Brochard some of his thinking existence, economic as well, thanks to the (honorable) inheritance she left him.[18] Still, Descartes may well have been the first to *doubt, not only the world but his mother*.[19]

What I wanted to write, for my less than Cartesian part, what I hope to have written, is something about mothers (not fathers, impossible as this still seems, judging by the reactions; we are not satiated yet by fathers, motherless fathers). As I shall reiterate, I wanted to write about mothers and *to* mothers as well, *for* mothers too, not just to mine. More important, primarily, I came to the realization I was writing *from* mothers and mothering. Doing so, I was not reaching for certainty, nothing immediately clear and distinct, but I did do my best to listen, to my mother and to other mothers. And I know that in this as well I have been, *as I will always be*, my mother's child, my mother's son. But I have not sought here to know or show myself, not even to expose or hide myself, a doubtful or dutiful, a cleverly inquisitive (much less an inquisitor) child. An original author, initiator of some future promise. In fact, I have not tried to show myself at all (I realize I am already breaking that rule and that I will again make one or two disclosures in what follows). What I hope to have done is grasp, or catch and betray, and really learn (as we all have or had to) something from mothers, learn what I have learned from mothers. And perhaps, again, *for* mothers too. This seems the least of all gestures to return, to turn to or repeat, to extend or even overextend, having been mothered, for having been mothered. For having all been mothered.

Were *we* to contend with this plural state of affairs, with *the plurality of mothers* ("A Kentucky of Mothers," as the poet Dana Ward writes),[20] with our having been mothered, over time, rather than inaugurate *our pertinacious stories of primordial beginnings* with the one mother who gives birth to the one child ("His Majesty the Baby"), we might then identify a missing element of political thought, of political experience, a broader political truth. We might rethink and even relive (perhaps relieve) motherhood, foreground *maternality* over natality. We might, in other words, *grow* and *accompany* mothers as they have us. Our mothers, ourselves, one could say, to borrow a phrase. For mothers—is this not obvious?—do much more than give birth. They do more than care for us and raise us. Mothers *are* more than that. Mothers *accompany* us. Over time. And time, yes, "time is a mother."[21] Which is why mothers accompany (anticipate and memorize, shape and relinquish, ignore or worse, with indelible consequences) our most essential needs, our raging wants, our most arbitrary desires. More or less well, yes? But for how long?

For how long, I ask. Is this a "biological," psychological, or technological question?[22] Or, assuming there is a difference, is it a historical question? What is the measure of time by which mothering—mothering and not conceiving—could or should be measured in time? Rather than argue with the psychologists and the psychoanalysts, the anthropologists and the historians, over the number, shape, or agency of "formative" years (or, God forbid, over the definition of life, fetal rather than maternal), I resolutely err on the side of time. Mothers and time. Mothers, even dead—or simply regretful—mothers, accompany us in time.[23]

In the time that remains, we might do so in our turn, linger otherwise, motherwise, with those who continue to dwell, for better or for worse and however unevenly, unequally, in those energetic zones of control and domination or else of silent and pained exteriority, of unviability even, vis-à-vis the political as it is still understood—or rather shrunken and skewed. As I try to describe it, I shall be reiterating that which we have been missing (God, and mothers, know at what rising cost) the maternal in the political, *the maternal as the political.*

On the Sovereignty of Mothers proposes that we think the political otherwise than paternal and patriarchal, otherwise than fraternal. We must rather think the political *as it has always been*: maternal. The book will proceed by way of three interconnected vectors, mobilized and redeployed and, judging by their canonical use and currency, indispensable, "public concepts," as Iris Murdoch wrote. These are: slavery, sovereignty, and the social contract. My three chapters, roughly divided along these entangled lines (after an introduction that expounds *maternal writing*) do not offer new definitions or systematic treatments of these contested and relational concepts—each a "political Pandora's box," as Joan Cocks explains.[24] There will be no "exploding received definitions of motherhood" either, but rather old-new elaborations, supplementary descriptions of multifariously rehearsed, if oddly wanting—and waning—notions.[25] Thus, guided by the biblical Hagar and Sarah, I recognize an uncertain but perduring dialectic—mother and slave—that undergirds the famous Hegelian pairing of master and slave and, more important, exceeds and complicates accepted maternal (and certainly familial) boundaries. I then go on to propose that, no less intrinsic to that entanglement of sovereignty and slavery, and, as it were, prior to the social contract, the sexual contract, and the racial contract, there is a *maternal contract*.[26] Such priority, which has little to do with nature, with "Mother Nature," cannot be confined to the family and has, in any case, everything to do with history (even if this must include natural history), which should signal the arbitrariness of beginnings and of foundations (I have nothing to say, therefore, about that isolate of origin and power called "mother-right" or matriarchy, that other—or not—origin story).[27] The maternal contract binds mother to mother, mother to slave, laterally and *transgenerationally*, as I shall explain. With it and intrinsic to it, I identify, in any case, a compelling opportunity to ponder maternal sovereignty, the sovereignty of mothers.[28]

I cannot emphasize enough that my aim is *descriptive*. The material—the maternal—I engage has long been there for all to recall or see, to witness and read. We have all been mothered, but this has hardly prevented us from ignoring that, or from elaborating theories and polities predicated on the most blatant, the most violent repression of that extended and necessary condition, as if it were some kind of expendable origin story. At this late point in time, my aim is descriptive, I say, which means—and this is no less crucial—that I have no interest in upholding the normative or prescriptive dimensions of the notions that guide me. This is not *The School for Good Mothers* and I am not advocating for (or against) any future, much less a reproductive one, nor am I concerned with demographic trends, much less demographic threats of whatever kind (none of them very convincing, if you ask me).[29] I am not after the nature, certainly not the essence, of mothers (nor do I seek to counter essentialism with some redemptive historicism). I propose no "new maternalism" and do not want "to foster the identity of 'women-as-mothers' and to establish the moral primacy of the family, and so the private realm of human life."[30] I have no desire either to glorify maternal ethics, or to pronounce on mothers as progressive or conservative (as if these words still meant something). I certainly have no wish to confine mothers to some natural bond, to a familial or national enclave, fated to domestic or other ethical, indeed, caring, or teaching realms, be these even temporary, exemplary. I am

not, in short, of the opinion that mothers *should* mother, however perfectly, however well enough.[31] I only know that they
have overwhelmingly done so, doing so still, and repeatedly
performing—and resisting too—the indispensable functions we
might acknowledge as maternal.

What I seek, then, is a better account of the abiding force of
mothers, a better description of maternal functions, the divisions
of maternal labor, of the conditions under which we have experienced and instituted (to invoke Rich again), preserved too, and
therefore *reproduced*, our collective existence (not only the reproduction of mothers, of the family, or of the labor force, to say
nothing of "the species")—over time.[32] Foregrounding mothers,
infinitely different and divided mothers and the divisions of
maternal labor, I seek to describe a distinct field, of different limits and divisions. For in order for collectives—I do insist on this
general and even generic term, to refer to that which has never
been equal nor reducible to "the" family, any family or community, any clan, tribe, race or religion, people or nation—to exist
and endure in time, there must be, there must have been, mothering. Within and across generation, no collective can last without mothering. Indeed, the very constitution and preservation,
the reproduction, over time, of the collective as a whole, of any collective as a site of unequal association and relation, of power and
preservation, is maternal.[33] Thus, whatever beginning or foundation we underscore and, more important, whatever means of
reproduction or whatever technology of reproduction, we consider (and yes, there are other such means, whether economic,
legal—norms and customs—social, or ritual),[34] these must be
transmitted and taught to, imprinted with—which is to say,

written and indeed reproduced onto—new members of the collective, any collective. Onto the polity and onto the world. In and over time.

Without mothers or mothering—the plural and difficult nature, meaning, and function of which this book endeavors to explore—there can be, in time, no collective, no political collective. There has not been such collective so far, even if each actually existing collective has (mostly) failed, that is, failed and denied its maternal functions, its maternal conditions; even if each has so very often, so very spectacularly, failed mothers—sometimes by glorifying them to perfection, other times by criminalizing, enslaving, and discarding them. What should be next, now that the fantasy of replacing mothers—persistently and exasperatingly, narrowly and violently, understood as little more than bodies conceiving (or not), pregnant (or not) and birthing (or aborting), and always as *individual* bodies—seems so obviously at hand, I leave for others to contemplate.[35] If time allows. If time remains.

"There must be, there must have been mothering," I wrote. The way one might say, "someone's got to do it," without wishing to linger on the condition, the unfreedom, of those confronting that "heaviest of social burdens" (Adrienne Rich) and fulfilling such unequal tasks and "opportunities."[36] *There has been mothering*, to be more precise, for we have all been mothered. *How and by whom* is part of what must be acknowledged, described, and reckoned with. And possibly, but this is another story, changed. Perhaps—"Don't produce and don't reproduce!"—even *ended*.[37]

I locate my argument in the neglect of the maternal, relegating it at best to "first things," to beginnings or foundations, most often familial or mythological foundations.[38] And I might as well express here my astonishment at the all-too-minor role mothers appear (or disappear) to play, the place that motherhood and mothering takes, in political thought (as opposed to personal or subjective or familial thought, strange and estranged zones of exception) and that even feminists (or psychoanalysts) have accorded motherhood in their political thinking—a thinking of the polity at large—let alone in their thinking of sovereignty.[39] Of sovereignty, not of choice. That astonishment, in any case, was a determining catalyst for the writing of this book.

"A clear and distinct idea of motherhood," I wrote in reference to Descartes. But who doesn't *know* mothers? Who fails to partake in the *certainty* of mothers? I will have occasion to clarify and underscore one more thing, which must be stated outright nevertheless. I write of mothers, *not of women*; of mothering, not of caring. Obviously—*obviously!!*—women have been mothers. Yet, equally *clear and certain* is the fact that not all women mother, nor are all mothers women. They—women, mothers—surely have extended a whole lot of care, "these activities which consist in bringing a concrete response to the needs of others—domestic labor, care, education, support and assistance, among others ... [that] have been performed overwhelmingly by women, if not by all women, or by certain people belonging to subaltern categories."[40] I repeat, then, that with and beyond care (I insist, more broadly, on *writing*), mothers have not always been women. Nor have women always (really, not *always*) fulfilled all maternal functions.[41] It is evidently right to ask about women's status and, indeed, to fight for freedom, equality, and power within the family and without, or within society at large in all its dimensions.

But these are different questions, I believe, than those that emerge when asking about mothers and mothering in the polity, about the political as maternal. A consideration of motherhood seems to me to require that the distinction between woman and mother be maintained (it has, of course), that women not be reduced to motherhood, nor that motherhood be equated with womanhood. That distinction must be acknowledged and preserved, and this for temporal, conceptual, and political reasons, which I shall also endeavor to make explicit. At stake is, perhaps, a historical distinction, moreover, one that was *enforced* (as the collapse of the distinction yet continues to be enforced in forcing women to mother) much earlier than—if certainly during—the ravages of Atlantic slavery that were clearly inflicted with singular cruelty.[42] That distinction (women, mothers) further implicates the color and gender lines that long defined, that still define, forms of domination and exploitation, the division of labor, means of production and of reproduction, as well as current geopolitical surges of surrogacy, reconsiderations of gender roles and assignments, or the artificial wombs (or the AI nurses or teachers) now being developed, no doubt, in corporate laboratories.

Mothers, then. For to claim that the political is maternal is also to ask—over time, that is—between the noun and the verb: Who are mothers? Who mothers? The answers, along with the indisputable giving and taking (if not always freely given) that mothering constitutes and reproduces, hardly means, should it not be obvious, that mothers have held the reins of power. Never simply so, nor mostly so. Certainly no more than have the workers or the slaves (those "belonging to subaltern categories" or worse), the masses or indeed the people (that other, better-touted sovereign). But oppression and domination, exploitation and enslavement, between slavery and sovereignty by way of denial, erasure, and murder, however relentless—these do not exhaust the essence or the existence of their "addressee" or subject, their function and significance. They do not *make* a polity, much less preserve it. Mothers do that. Over time.

It was at the kind invitation of Jonathan Boyarin and Deborah Starr that I presented, in October 2022, three lectures entitled "The Sovereignty of Mothers" as part of the Messenger Lecture Series and the Jewish Studies Program at Cornell University. As I complete the revisions of the lectures into a book, I am most grateful to my hosts and to the audience as I am to Diane Rubenstein, Gerard Aching, Tracy McNulty, Jill Frank, Philip Lorenz, Tanzeen Doha, Re'ee Hagay, and Ayla Cline.

I thank Wendy Lochner for her unwavering support. Along with Jennifer Crewe, the editors and editorial board of Columbia University Press and two anonymous, but discerning, readers, this book has felt like the easier thing in impossible times. And I thank Susan Pensak for her impeccable editing.

In more ways than I otherwise explain, this book was written to, for and from my mother. But I am also searching for a way to register my gratitude to the mothers I am fortunate to have known—a better way than the mere listing of names. For now, among mothers and othermothers, I wish to single out Joëlle Marelli, in particular, along with Elisabeth Apter, Gertraud Auer Borea d'Olmo, Talal Asad, Nadine Barros-Ichai, Francesc Burgos, Ronit Chacham, Leila Farsakh, Ani Garmiryan, David Kishik, Beatrice Marovich, Zehra Mehdi, Marc Nichanian, Avner Ofrath,

Omar Ortiz, Mariella Pandolfi, Paola Petrić, Amnon Raz-Krakotzkin, Jacqueline Rose, Ruth Tsoffar, Carol Marie Webster, Netta Yerushalmy, and Elleni Centime Zeleke for essential conversations and lifetimes of learning, reading, and mothering. Last but not least, Irit Levy—the one and the many.

ON THE SOVEREIGNTY
OF MOTHERS

INTRODUCTION

THE MOTHER IN ME

FOR BETTER OR WORSE, the writing of a book has often been figured as a kind of birth, or birth giving, the rearing of and caring for a child.[1] Metaphor, substitute, or violent appropriation, at times the expression of an exclusive alternative—*aut libri aut liberi*—one might nevertheless grant the reverse as well, namely, that motherhood is a form of writing in the world.[2] And perhaps of the world. Text instead of context. Text together with context. Preparing these lectures, writing this book, in daily conversations with my mother (a ritual so ancient now I can no longer date it), I certainly feel I have an answer to the question of whether mothers write. I do not mean, not only, *writing mothers*, as some clearly are or have been writers in the more obvious sense.[3] Rather more generally, it seems to me indisputable that mothers, that is, mothers who do not write books, poems, or doctoral theses (and those mothers, too, who do not have to struggle with or, indeed, renounce motherhood, in order to write), these mothers, all mothers, are not only written or written about.[4] They themselves write. Which means that mothers are not to be read, heard, remembered, or understood as some distant, or absent origin, as contexts for the texts we, we who have been mothered, read and write—or are. Mothers rather multifariously demonstrate their capacity—and perhaps it is already the sovereignty—to inscribe themselves and others onto the bodies of their children and well beyond, onto the body politic, the polity and the world.

MATERNAL WRITING

"Is there such a thing as the writing mother's fantasy?" Susan Suleiman asks. I should know—is what I would say. To an extent I can only partly fathom, I am my mother's fantasy (and no doubt her worst fears too). I am certainly my mother's fantasy writer. You might well imagine then, that, *together*, we write a kind of translation.[5] Or else, like Octavia Butler, writer of mothers extraordinaire, we write speculative fiction (I do wish we could have written *Kindred*, or a version thereof). Which is another way for me to say that I am structured like my mother's languages, the dream of her existence, the stuff of her unconscious. Mother-work is work. It is hard work, *dependency work*, as Eva Feder Kittay powerfully puts it.[6] Which is to say that it is economic work, yes, and also social work, political work (over time, mothers bring new members into the collective, into the polity). Yet mother-work is also dream-work, the dream-work of the other, the dream-work of others.[7] Is a child not the fulfillment of a wish? A process of displacement and distortion, condensation and more—is not a mother?[8] Could my mother have written this? Did she not, in fact, write? What of her dreams, of their (inseparable, Freud says) interpretations? Could she have written otherwise? Had she a room of her own, would she have written a different book, her own book?

My mother tells few stories about herself. She does not remember many details about her childhood and even since, except for her having failed to acquire a memory, she says, or insufficiently interrogated her mother's.[9] She, who doesn't know English well enough to read my work, did remember, as I embarked on this project, that the very first paper I presented, decades ago, at an academic conference was a reading of mothers (in the biblical book 1 Samuel). But what my mother conveyed and transmitted, what she molded and shaped, goes well beyond her conscious memories. Or mine. I therefore carry—as she did and does—"an effect of reproduction, a trace of maternity."[10] I am, in other words, not that line which, between two isolated points on a blank plane, leads from cradle to grave; a different, palimpsestic geometry, time, relations and functions of the imperfect page (albeit one among the pages) upon which my mother has inscribed herself. And perhaps I should already say: her selves.

I speak of her, for the most part, in the singular and in the possessive too. As if it were possible. Or intelligible. I will continue to do so, without contradicting, I think, the arguments I have begun to announce, the insistence I place on plurality, the plurality of mothers.[11] There is surely something partial and even misleading about this singular. There always is, is what I am trying to say. Along with my siblings, for instance, I was also raised, as my mother and her siblings were, by her mother. I mean this in more than one, obvious, way. My grandmother, about whom I shall have more to say later (for she too was many), accompanied us, all of us, and does so still, many years after her death. As I write of and with my mother, then, I cannot but acknowledge that I am, that we are, she and I, the shifting and encrypted surfaces that have been prepared and imprinted, "an indelible mother-scripture," a book she has (been) written.[12] A book we have (been) written.

As I mentioned earlier, it is undoubtedly the case that a great number of sons, male writers, have written (instead of) their mother—"Mother, can't you see I'm writing?"—playing with their mother's body as Roland Barthes infamously put it. And quite a few daughters too. What I am intending, however, is different. Not that I am writing the book my mother would have written, but rather (or perhaps also) that I *am* the book she has written. More broadly, and more generally, I want to claim, or rather acknowledge, that there is a *general* writing, *a maternal writing*, that does not take, does not have to take, the recognizable form of a book (though it still has to be read).[13] Maternal writing does not even have to take the form of what we call writing in a narrow sense of that term. What this means is that, as I speak, since I speak, I speak the words of my mother, the words of her mother, words made flesh, if you wish, and the (m)other way around, which we breathed day in and day out. The words, and also the silences, you are hearing (now reading), the words (the bodies and the souls) you are missing, are also words I have *rendered* to my mother; words I have tried, still try, to listen to and hear, also to speak, write, and read to her—albeit in another tongue, from another mother tongue. In what follows, I therefore pursue and endeavor to voice words and things that I have heard and learned, perform gestures and motions already repeated by my mother and hers, haunted or inhabited, inherited, negotiated in defiance of her or that she had learned to avoid or withhold (with and against her, from her and for her). This is where I might speak of inheritance and of tradition (which always meant selection, rejection, interpretation, resignification), of generations, and neither of heredity nor determinism.[14] I speak of the mother in me.[15]

An allobiography, then? Better yet, a *metrography* (from the Greek *mētēr*, mother) in which I shall touch upon mothers and be touched by them, more or less incisively, by the grammars and the emotions (love and language, love of language) that my mother inscribed and reinscribed, gave and taught me and rehearsed together with me. Year after year, for better and worse, my mother has impressed me, impressed her changing and shifting selves upon me, as she impresses me still and differently. My mother, I should clarify, has always struck me as being divided, as being many: "decentered, split, or doubled in several ways."[16] Intimations of incisions and divisions that include loving or hating me, rejecting me even, pressing me, softly and harshly, hurting or comforting me, preparing or exposing me (do I blame her? I did, I did, of course, blame my mother—for everything).[17] Most often, she cajoled me, habituated me, and—most important? for her, anyway—she fed me (even "the hunger strike of the anorexic," Jacques Lacan thought, long enough to convince me at least, "signifies a psychological return to the maternal breast").[18] Mother and mouth (as Maggie Nelson puts it, we "are alive today . . . because someone once adequately policed [our] mouth exploring").[19] Mother and mouth, yes, words and things, edible and inedible, actions and reactions, domestic idioms and languages of the state or of the tradition, musical themes, and psychic impressions—all of which my mother herself inherited, all of which she learned, or learned to learn, *from her mother*. All of which she suffered or reworked, translated and expanded—upon me—often unwittingly; all of which she distributed evenly, if still unequally, upon my siblings and me; all of which she also concealed, those languages she knew and chose not to teach me, for instance, languages she knew and those she did not learn. Or forgot. Or denied.

I do not write *for* my mother, therefore, nor do I speak in her stead, not even in her "defense."[20] And though she does read me and lose me in translations, I do not seek to represent her either.[21] For my mother has known to present and represent herself, to me and to others, through me and through others. More or less well. Over time. She has been content, at any rate, within lingering limits, to conduct for herself her own exercises in power and persuasion, her own writing. In this case too, therefore, "it is all persuasion and education," affection and domination.[22] It has certainly been a "training of the affections," as John Stuart Mill had it. But hardly of those only. And then, the negotiations. I am not my mother ("It is not a case of identification with the mother," although I genuinely wonder sometimes).[23] Still, I do write *to* my mother and perhaps *for* her after all. Truly and mostly, though, I write *from* her. And so my words, which are and are not her words, shall remain those I have received from her, diverted, distorted, or extracted from her, fought over with her, used, learned with and against her. Am I my mother's keeper? Dedicating these words to her, I know I am the memory of her, as she is the memory of her mother and more.[24] An embodied memory, an "ensouled body."[25] She is also the memory of me, knowing what I do not know of myself, and not only by that strange and singular transitivity whereby, like most mothers, *she has lived my life from the beginning.* For months, for years, my mother lived a life I cannot claim as strictly mine (a deferred chapter: mothers and property), with no consciousness to speak of, no consciousness to speak. Our finitude: our mothers know us and live us over time—time out of mind—they read and mark the rhythms of our moods and bodies, better than we ourselves.[26] Mothers and time. For I do not think this stops at the early years, even if I too remember things of her, for her. I am, I have always been and will always be "in memory of her."[27] I am my mother's spirit—I mean, my mother's writing. Which means *I am in her absence* (the way one used to say, "in her danger") as she was, and remains, in mine. An erasure too, which cannot be helped, I think. A *logos* always already orphaned from its mother.[28] Or mothers.

Now, the following has been well rehearsed. The body, real and virtual, is a surface or space of inscription, as is the soul, the self.[29] Writing about mothers, writing about my mother, I have been repeatedly amazed by the persistence of her impressions, her love, her dreams, wishes, and questions, by the writing force, the "social force," you might say, and yes, "the weak messianic force" or indeed the sovereignty differentially exerted by mothers (and not only Jewish mothers) upon the bodies and tongues of their children.[30] Even absent or dead mothers—so many of them Black mothers today—those violently denied their very motherhood, do leave a mark and an inscription, indelible gaps, in fact, or undecipherable traces, most often unchosen and even forced, on their children, the bodies and souls of the living, the dead and the orphaned.[31] And—*partus sequitur ventrem*—those of children born into slavery too.[32] But mothers, figured since time immemorial as fields to be plowed, are themselves made of ink and of blood, makers of ink and blood. "I made the ink," says Sethe in Toni Morrison's *Beloved*. "He couldn't have done it if I hadn't made the ink."[33] Mothers are made of surfaces and of erasures, of seams and of folds—a history of writing that remains less to be written, perhaps, than attended to and read. And so I shall speak here of bodies strained, often to the breaking point, bodies pained and enslaved, bodies even tortured, and of other imprints as well, of the literal and phantasmatic, the social, cultural, or racial formations to which mothers surrender and resist, that mothers inherit and transmit, endorse, oppose, or resignify, that they read and write and rewrite—that they translate—on their own flesh, as they themselves are written.

I shall speak of mothers, if I may be allowed to insist, from and to mothers, and always with mothers as well. Of mothers and less of children, and certainly not of The Child. Of the past and present of mothers and of mothering.[34] "The pragmatics of motherhood,"as Nancy Scheper-Hughes puts it.[35] I shall surrender to an old-new lexical movement, a paleonymic commitment to name mothers and mothering.[36] I shall do so with the help of the usual, and unusual, experts. My mother herself, my mother first of all, the many mothers she has been, as well as those I have known and whom I continue to learn from. Some very close (my grandmother, my wife, my sisters, my friends), some distant (the mother of my children, other mothers I have known, or disappointed, others I was disappointed by); all of whom I admire, if differently, differentially. Many of these mothers and othermothers—and perhaps inevitably all of them—are also "fictitious," literary, or, better yet, "mythological" (who isn't?). At some key juncture in this journey, at any rate, I was persuaded to follow, to repeat or rehearse, the maternal paths powerfully treaded by Jacqueline Rose's *Mothers*, by Elissa Marder's *The Mother in the Age of Mechanical Reproduction*, and by Andrew Parker, *The Theorist's Mother*. But I learned from others, from other mothers, from psychiatrists and psychoanalysts, anthropologists and philosophers, writers and critics, white feminists and Black feminists, womanists and nonfeminists too, even from misogynists, no doubt, none of whom could quite *own,* nor exhaust, the subject of mothers, mothers as objects—mothers as subjects.[37] I myself make no claim to expertise. I hold no diploma in "mother studies," not from my alma mater, or any other institution of higher learning. *Of mothers born, raised, and accompanied*, I merely confess to seeking the measure, the expanse, of a field, the maternal field.

What is it that we all say, after all, when we say "mother?" What singularity, what plurality, what generality or universality—what certainty—transpires thereby? What ground opens and closes, and what fictions govern? Allow me to begin again, and not, as it may seem, at the beginning. I am fifty-nine years old as I write this and I have been in conversations with my mother for my entire life ("how difficult it is to draw the temporal boundary of the dependency relationship between mother and child"!).[38] Even from an ocean away, I speak with my mother every day. I am, you could say, a mama's boy. Or perhaps I am a "Mother-addict."[39] For what else could I do? What else could I be? I speak with my mother, who has thus accompanied me, in word and in deed, in sickness and in health, and in endless pain and laughter, my entire existence.

I began to think, more or less earnestly, about mothers, I believe, when I realized that I was dreading the end of this accompaniment. I was and remain terrified of my mother's death. Which also means that I do not have, could never have had, another sense of death, of that death I call mine (as if it were), no other image—I do not say "understanding"—of it than the loss of her, the end, if it is one, of her companionship.[40] The mother in me may be read as resisting this end, a melancholy motif perhaps (dream work and mourning work). In a more erudite context, one would not write another mourning diary (Roland Barthes, Albert Cohen, Ocean Vuong) but instead ponder the maternal introject I mournfully carry always and already, that every "I" carries, thinking or unthinking (Descartes!), or so it seems to me, more or less early, more or less brutally. There are other introjections, no doubt, other accompaniments, yet the introjection of that vast domain we call the whole of social life (present or absent, the mother) may be poorly understood if we refer to it, as Abraham and Torok do, as "the non-mother." Is that domain not, after all, another form, another translation, of "the motherhood of the mother?"[41] We all lose our mother, Saidiya Hartman suggested, the body of our mother, or else *we lose our maternality*, and indeed fail to, even as some of us deny ever having had one. Do male children, in particular, ever settle the question of *having* rather than *being* their mother? Do not all children, all mothers, mourn their mother—or motherhood—or do they fail to? "The literalization of anatomy not only proves nothing . . . it is a literalizing restriction" of identity.[42]

It is, in any case, the nature of the companionship, that social, nay, political form, the nature and form of what binds me to my mother, what binds her mothers, her selves, to me, or us, to them for better and worse, for life and death, through life and after death (that is: in time) that I seek to understand in this book.

MATERNAL FUNCTIONS

Exceptionally or not, my mother struggled and played with, she fulfilled, she had to fulfill, an extraordinary number of *maternal functions* (Sara Ruddick distinguishes birth giving from mothering and lists "preservation, growth, and social acceptability," later adding or rephrasing these as "protection, nurturance, and training").[43] If mother is indeed a verb, it is because its conjugations are endlessly plural. I have already indicated that this is true of my mother as well. I will continue to underscore and endeavor to illustrate this plurality, appending to those verbs Sarah Knott explores in the English language, verbs such as conceiving, carrying, birthing, feeling, feeding, fearing, cleaning and cleaning after, changing, sleeping (and not sleeping), molding, smiling, clothing, holding, caressing, playing, measuring, waiting, pressing and impressing, listening, leaving, gendering, worrying, bearing, crying, healing, singing, soothing, talking, laughing, training, responding, guilting, regulating, screaming, relinquishing, relating and socializing, mediating, repeating and repeating some more, becoming and otherwise changing, and changing still.[44] Over time. There are many more to be added. Or subtracted. I will insist, at any rate, on *writing*, on a general writing that is, as I said, a maternal writing, that includes and erases, that repeats and reiterates all those verbs and their tenses that mothering is and does. Early on, by way of a literal instance, my mother taught my siblings and I to read and write. She did this early indeed, and well before we ever went to school, even before nursery school (or the proximately named *école maternelle*). Like her mother, like many mothers, my mother conveyed language and tradition, habits and phobias, tongues and idioms, rhetorical habits (irony, sarcasm, avoidance, and relentless attentiveness), knowledge and emotions. Their absence and silence too. True to the advice of experts of various persuasions (books, magazines, and radio), in any case, she taught us more than that. I might venture, with all due respect to my father, that my mother fathered us too (I would grant that he mothered us as well sometimes, if not *as well*). She certainly taught me how to be (and bear) a father. More or less well. Or a brother among brothers and sisters (there is another book folded in this sentence). Whence I speak as well. And write. Very much so.

And so I shall write of mothers, literally, laterally, and, as it were, unilaterally. I shall insist and repeat the word and verb *mother* in order to underscore the significance of *repetition*, of iteration, and therefore of writing, of mothering. I shall write of (or with) the innumerable gestures and words, the countless repeated instances and situations—the endless separations too—that mothering has implied and continues to imply, to apply and inscribe, well beyond familial or domestic spheres, however conceived. Elaborating on "the Law of the Mother," Juliet Mitchell accordingly finds and foregrounds "forbiddance" and "inducing reality" to that list of maternal functions.[45] And Cynthia Willett beautifully summarizes it all (as if that too were possible) when she writes—in the singular still, but with impeccable timing—that "mother and infant choreograph the boundaries of the real."[46] Mother is indeed a verb. Across the maternal field, it is emphatically conjugated in the plural always, endlessly written and reiterated (some maternal gestures, Donald Winnicott says somewhere, are literally repeated thousands of times, though he does not linger on the impossible, on "the psychic toll of repetitiously attempting to perform activities beyond one's ability").[47]

Thus, the work that my mother *did and did again and does very much still* would certainly satisfy both ends of Friedrich Engels's assertion that "the production and reproduction of immediate life [has] a twofold character: on the one side, the production of the means of existence, of food, clothing and shelter and the tools necessary for that production; on the other side, the production of human beings themselves."[48] My mother, the original economist,[49] did that and more. She did much more than perform and fulfill her economic or so-called biological functions (go ahead and argue about base and superstructure). She certainly did more than fulfill a natural, familial, or domestic role. To repeat, maternal functions are many and changing, but the vast field of their inscription, what I am calling the maternal field, is also broader and wider than has been granted. As I reflect on maternal writing and on the divisions of maternal labor, I shall therefore speak of *reproduction* in that broad sense. Not only the reproduction of mothering, of the family, or of the species, but an endless series of functions, social and political functions, the endless writing that has been overwhelmingly performed, repeated, and reiterated – effaced as well – on the world stage by mothers and othermothers throughout ages and villages and among all cultures. My mother is and is not different, therefore. Does not mothering evidently mean "preparing [children] for a world larger than the family?"[50] Ambivalently embraced by and, no less ambivalently, embracing the collective, the community or polity, or else that famous "nanny state" that France has figured itself ("Labourage et pâturage sont les deux mamelles dont la France est alimentée"),[51] my mother showed and introduced, she mediated the family, the neighborhood, the people, and the country (peoples and countries) and the world to us. She did so slowly, preparing us for the world. What mother could refrain from doing that? My mother introduced us to the world, formally and informally, carefully made it our playground before it could expand and materialize further. She also kept the world at bay. We always had, in any case, carefully to partake of that proverbial village, that society to which we belonged or not, that collection of fragmented and vanishing collectives, that maternal field.

With my mother and thanks to her we were (equal and unequal) siblings, nieces and nephews, cousins, friends, a constant opportunity she seized to teach us and impart a sense of justice. With her and thanks to her, there were other mothers, grandmothers and grandfathers, aunts and uncles, all of whom we learned to love and relate to (and with whom, from whom, we witnessed, mothers' multifarious dependency work). With her and thanks to her, we had family repeatedly and lavishly over for Shabbat and holidays, or else for no particular (if often stressful) reason. We also had friends, we had boyfriends and girlfriends we could hang out with and receive at home. I would not say that my sisters, otherwise mothered, always received the same treatment. Not at all (they became different mothers too). In what she said and in what she did ("do as I say, . . . ") my mother obviously repeated and reproduced (and innovated on) mother patterns, on gender patterns too. She sometimes disapproved of our friendships, but we could not have had them, have them still, so thickly without her love, her understanding and support. Ever the school teacher, she taught us about sex (there was little explicit talk of it, but much encouragement for us boys, and yes, massively different, albeit regulative as well, for my sisters). She obviously, if also obscurely, defined or at least imprinted my gendering and sexuality, not only preferences, along with my relationship to swear words (she never used any in our presence) and to sex-talk, and my general, intimate bashfulness.

In whatever smothered words, Jewish words, my mother also lived and transmitted exile and estrangement.[52] Worlds and habits, peoples and traditions forgotten or lost. She taught us about death, sustained and accompanied us when it struck (she also prevented us, boys and girls, from going to cemeteries for as long as she could). In more than one way, my mother also saved and rescued me. From death. She did that and told me that as well. Very, very early. She told me about my death, my near-death. For as long as I can remember, I have known that, but for her (maternal, divine) intervention, I came close to dying as an infant. I was ill, and she cared for me and fed me, she cured me through sleepless nights, as the doctors soon confirmed. "He would have died," they said. You could conclude that she gave me life twice. Or said that she did. Or else that she really gave me life and also gave me death, the tears and the prayers to say death, the memory of it, the instant of my death.[53] Later, on the way to writing, my mother allowed me to leave, my own private Exodus, face or escape other dangers and other revelations, take my distances from her again. And again. Over the years, there were letters, long letters. Thus my mother tutored and instructed me, schooled me, having tirelessly spoken to my teachers, sustained and encouraged me in my emotional and scholarly learning. Through the years, my mother loved me and taught me. She wrote me and wrote to me. At times I thought she erased me. She certainly fought and opposed me. She does this still, thank God and bless her soul: she listens always, affirms and accepts, responds and talks, teaches, disputes, and fights. Oh mother, does she fight!

She accompanies me. She calls me and calls to me always, like Heidegger's conscience. Like Heidegger's mother.[54] And that call, my mother's call to me, is for the most part "something which we ourselves," she and I, "have neither planned nor prepared for nor voluntarily performed, nor have we ever done so." This *writing* that I am and follow (*suis / suivre,* as Derrida had it),[55] this mother that I am and follow, is the mother in me. More than that, for my mother's call reaches out—through it and with it, someone or something calls, which does so "against our expectations and even against our will." By now, "the call undoubtedly does not come from someone else who is with me in the world." Not simply so. My mother's call is rather one (or many) that "comes from me and yet from beyond me and over me," from my mother and yet from beyond her, from her and over her.[56]

As I meditate on texts and contexts, on the calling and the writing of mothers, I know I am the text that my mother authored ("I call the mother the author of life . . . the author of my life," writes Muraro).[57] This is one reason to speak of authorial sovereignty and, more broadly, of maternal sovereignty, as I will later in this book. For now, adapting Sara Ahmed, I might venture that, if our texts are indeed worlds, it is because they are made of maternal materials.[58] At the same time—what is an author?—I am made of other cloths too, answering to other or older authorities, often, to othermothers, responding in other mother tongues, to other mother calls. Whatever I hear, whatever I learn, and whatever I write and write with or against, I know that my mother prepared me, and that I never strayed as far as it seemed, or as far as I thought. Or that she thought and felt.

And my father? He is next, or after next, as the Prophet assured. He is very much here, or there, between the lines, if not behind the curtain. And so I want to conclude this introduction by acknowledging, reiterating, that I am also more (and also much less) than the text my mother has written. You could say that I am also one, if I am one, of her writing instruments. I don't mean anything phallic here, although love and desire—and, yes, gender—will have had everything to do with it. With me and through me, and certainly beyond me, my mother made her mark, one of her many marks onto the world. Which is finally to say that mothers—for I obviously do not speak only of my own mother here—have "used" their children as writing instruments *onto the world at large*. These have been male or female, blunt or refined, compliant or resistant, ephemeral and permanent, and anywhere in between. As "mothers of the race" or as "mothers of the nation," mothers of the tribe, the religion, or the species (as if we could tell the difference), mothers have written and they have been written. They have been glorified and confined, used and abused, loved, rejected, and negated as makers and producers of future citizens.[59] Rather than authors or authorities, it is true, they have often served, been made to serve—yes, serve—as mere typists, at best copyists, of writing and living regimes, writing systems and so-called mother tongues.[60] In this, the task of their translations, mothers have often had, or seemed to have, too restricted a space, too little or rather too opaque an impact to measure.[61] Still, mothers have written. Within and also beyond their intentions (and against them too), they have translated themselves onto their children, in and onto the family, the village, and beyond, further onto the world—taking the measure of each. They have written the world with and onto (and sometimes without) their children. This is not a metaphor and certainly not one reducible to any nature, or to the threshold of birth, which has too long defined *the* mother (singular), the certainty of the mother, in legal discourse and practice. With many more thresholds—lethal ones too—the world is fuller than this. It is fuller of mothers and of maternal inscriptions. And of maternal silences, absences. It is full of maternal writing. There is much to read, then, which is why a crucial question that will occupy and guide me has to do with the limits and the nature, the technological and political nature, of this field of writing, this field of transmission and of translation, this field of repetition and of reproduction, which I have begun to describe. What are the limits and expanses of the maternal field? How many maternal functions? How many mothers?

Chapter One

MOTHER AND SLAVE

IT TAKES A VILLAGE to raise a child.

We have all heard this common-place, which may or may not derive from that proverbial African saying.[1] We certainly know that it does indeed take the arduous and dedicated labor (one may more precisely say, if such could be heard or remembered, the *service*—as in public service—and arguably the servitude as well) of a whole lot of people, past and present. It takes necessary effort and support along with indispensable resources. It takes time, for a child, for *children*, to become adults who partake of the life of said village. But what, then, is a village? What kind of shared grouping and organized collective, what kind of tribe, what kind of regime or constitution is a village, a community or polity?[2] And what does it take, if it takes a village, to become a mother? It seems obvious that, much like Simone de Beauvoir had it with regard to women, one is not *born* a mother. One *becomes* a mother. Yet, being born *to* a mother, does one also and thereby (not) become a mother? Does *one*? As Jacqueline Rose asks, "to whom or what exactly is a woman giving birth?"[3] To whom indeed? And to how many? Over what length of time? Still focused primarily on birth, psychiatrists argue that "what a woman gives birth to in her mind is not a new human being, but a new identity: the sense of being a mother."[4] An abyssal logic—and computation. How many does this make, after all, and how many does it take? And when? When to start counting? And for how long? At birth, we are repeatedly told, but which now? What does that second birth, that "psychological birth" and obviously protracted, transformative becoming, entail, whom does it implicate, whom does it obligate and since when?[5] What other beginnings and what extended temporalities, what (dis)abilities, what maternal melancholies, what labor and what travails, what service or servility?[6] What work of life and, too often still, of death, what mind and what village, indeed, what *motherings* (what mothering of mothers) are carried and hidden under the image we still hold of *the one mother giving birth,* not only the lone or single mother, but—stranger, stronger and deeper than that faith in the one God of monotheism—the one and unique mother, the singular mother in and of that plural and proverbial village?

In what follows I shall be arguing—and I do say arguing—that becoming-mother involves much more than birthing and more than rearing; more than one mother, in other words, a division of maternal labor and a plurality of maternal functions.[7] This should be uncontroversial enough, not to say outrightly banal. Still, by mothering, I shall mean two things for now. First, that (perhaps too obvious) sense of an individual giving birth and/or raising a child (that is, one child at least, often more, sometimes less, if the pregnancy does not reach full term or if the child—or the mother—does not survive). Second, mothering as becoming-mother, a collective, protracted, and really interminable, a nego-tiated movement of (dis)abilities, an obviously transgenera-tional process of successful and less successful stages, of completion, incompletion, and also of devastation, all of which implicate (and cannot but implicate) mothers and othermothers. It does therefore take a village.[8] You might already conclude that I am evoking Adrienne Rich's distinction between experience and institution, and you would not really be wrong.[9] Still (and far from a conclusion, the beginning of political wisdom), if it takes a vil-lage, it is because motherhood always already constitutes "a certain kind of multi-person relationship," as Enid Balint explained.[10] It is also because mothers, whatever they become, are thereby and necessarily many. Mothers, to put it differently, must themselves be mothered. Mothers—everything it takes to become-mother, indeed, to mother—are a village.

Otherwise put: a village (a people or a polity, if we switch from a Latin to a Greek idiom) represents less what it did for Henry Maine, namely, "a midway point . . . between kinship and local-ity" or "the pure doubling of kinship and locality."[11] A village or polity (and not only the obvious mother-city, or *mētropolis*) is not quite "the forgotten land of the mother and mothers" either, which Siri Hustvedt evokes, as if quoting from *The Great Mother* (even if Hustvedt is right that there lies "a territory Western cul-ture has studiously repressed, suppressed, or avoided").[12] A vil-lage is rather—a mother. A village, a collective, must mother. In fact, a village *does* mother mothers—more or less well, more or less poorly, often terribly, unspeakably so. It must do so in order to maintain itself in time. It seems therefore high time for us to heed Jacqueline Rose as she proposes to "take as a model for our social as well as psychological well-being the complex, often painful reality of motherhood," which is indeed "not quite the same as suggesting mothers should rule the world, but it is close."[13] What this means is that beyond and through (but not necessarily before) the paternal or patriarchal and the fraternal, beyond primordial beginnings or founding fathers, beyond the familiar play of status and contract, and finally beyond the all-too expected practices of care—*the political is, in ways we have yet to understand, maternal.*[14]

Mothers—where else would one begin? And yet, I have already taken some distance from the notion that mothers are rightly or adequately construed as origins, or as primordial beginnings.[15] Here, I want to add what might appear as a late coordinate in the long history of mothering, or perhaps it is rather a reminder of a structure, the organization, of mothering, of the plurality of mothers. A reminder indeed, a maternal memory and, most strikingly, an image that, from under James Baldwin's pen, flashed up in a moment of danger, though it has left little trace and no commentary I could find.[16]

The "so-called American Negros," writes Baldwin wryly in *The Fire Next Time,* have a "great advantage," that "of having never believed that collection of myths to which white Americans cling." Black Americans, Baldwin goes on to explain, "know far more about white Americans than that," they know far more than the myths white Americans tell themselves. "It can almost be said, in fact, that they know about white Americans what parents—or, anyway, mothers—know about their children."[17] Such is the maternal image that seized or captured me, in turn, a striking instance of a "general and pansexual maternity," which defines the knowing perspective blacks have had on whites, the position they have occupied, the functions they have served.[18] The perspective, the position, the functions—one might have to say, with Maya Angelou, the blackness—of mothers.[19] Baldwin's stunning take on the American experiment is grounded in a historical and sociological fact, the measure of which is difficult, perhaps impossible, to fathom. During and after slavery, "the afterlife of slavery" (in Saidiya Hartman's striking phrase), in the opaque and protracted "temporality of enslavement" (as Jennifer Nash puts it) and for generations upon generations to this very day, an untold number of white children have been mothered, raised and cared for, by black women, by Black and brown mothers, those Joy James calls "captive maternals."[20] Today still, "the relationship between white mothers and mothers of color is repeating an age-old history, especially in the U.S., as undocumented migrants take care of the children of white middle-class mothers."[21] Especially, but by no means only, in the United States of America.

Baldwin's striking image is, as Walter Benjamin might have seen, fraught with danger, a danger that "affects both the content of the tradition and its receivers" since "the same threat hangs over both: that of becoming a tool of the ruling classes," a tool for those Baldwin identifies as white.[22] Well beyond the (more than legitimate) attention that transatlantic slavery has attracted (and also failed to attract), the image speaks of memory and of forgetting, of what "made the working class forget both its hatred and its spirit of sacrifice, for both are nourished by the image of enslaved ancestors rather than that of liberated grandchildren."[23] Otherwise nourishing, Baldwin's image thus speaks of an exception that has long been the rule. It speaks of Blackness, and of slavery, Atlantic slavery. It speaks of the Blackness of mothers and of "the long-standing conditions of the ordinary," rather than of a newly framed crisis.[24] Between history and ontology, Baldwin evokes a distinct tradition, one that teaches us about mother and slave. It is this lesson, this tradition, that governs everything I shall have to say.

HAGAR AND MONOTHEISM

"These things are being taken figuratively," writes Saint Paul in Galatians 4. This is a lesser known Paul I want to invoke here. It is, as always, a political Paul, one who understands much about the *polis* but also, if there is a difference, something about mothers. In this passage, in any case, Paul foregrounds, or institutes, a deep and significant repository of maternal imagery, and even conceives of himself as a mother; Paul, Beverly Gaventa underscores, is here better thought of as "our mother Saint Paul."[25] And he does accompany us still. Indeed, having just turned to the Galatians as his "dear children, for whom I am again in the pains of childbirth," Paul goes on to teach and explain the law, to explain the figures or allegories of the law he himself deploys.[26] Enter the city and the country, or as Augustine will rephrase and further popularize, on the basis of the same prooftext, enter the two cities.[27] Enter Hagar and Sarah.

"The women," Paul says, "represent two covenants. One covenant is from Mount Sinai and bears children who are to be slaves: This is Hagar. Now Hagar stands for Mount Sinai in Arabia and corresponds to the present city of Jerusalem, because she is in slavery with her children. But the Jerusalem that is above is free, and she is our mother." Paul is quite clear that both women are, as Fethi Benslama rightly insists, "two figures of the maternal" (Hagar is clearly said to "bear children"), yet only one of them is called mother.[28] Paradoxically, she—Sarah—remains here unnamed, though she is called, and only she is called, mother. There is here a remarkable echo of Romans 25 ("I will call them my people, which were not my people; and her beloved, which was not beloved"; and see Hosea 2), for Paul calls only her "mother" who is, he says, *our* mother, just as he declares here that we, we who are free, "we are not children of the slave woman, but of the free woman." Sarah, the free woman, is that mother who is called mother, whereas Hagar, that mother who is not a mother, is called "slave."

Was Hagar servant or slave? Was Hagar mother or slave? Could she (not) be? In Genesis 16 and 21, Hagar is identified by way of two different Hebrew words: *shifhah* and *amah*, the distinction between the two remaining obscure or irrelevant, and does not, for the most part, register in translation.[29] Only the Vulgate will deploy two words when translating Paul, namely, *serva* and *ancilla*.[30] Whatever the lexical difference in and across languages, both terms have surely come to evoke service, servitude, and slavery.

Now, the numerous debates over the nature and historicity of slavery as well as the historical onset of what we call race have, to some extent, contended with the Bible and its role.[31] The single most translated text in the history of mankind, this great mother of texts, has generated and provided endless material and resources for the political imagination and for political thought—often of the worst kind. A kind of exuberant, even chaotic, rejoinder to the foundational, and systematic, theorizations of Ancient Greece, the Bible is itself a political battlefield, an unwieldy and uncontainable collection of words, concepts, and ideas that, by now ubiquitous if often unrecognizable, challenges epistemic and generic constraints (law, history, narrative, politics, and of course "religion") along with any attempt to control its meaning, its political meaning. From the nature of the human by way of the right to inheritance to the constitution of a collective ("The Hebrew Republic" as Eric Nelson called it),[32] from the form of rule (divine or patriarchal, legal, monarchical, tyrannical) to the inevitability of transgression (Eve, Cain, the golden calf), rebellion (Moses, Korah), and fratricidal war (Cain, again, but also Judah and Israel, the Maccabees), all the way to the possibility of freedom and the desire for (and against) emancipation (the fleshpots of Egypt), and including the meaning of meaning, the Bible continues to permeate and affect debates on sexuality and reproduction ("Be fruitful and multiply"), abortion, and, inevitably, the family as well as, evidently, motherhood. Most famously, perhaps, the Bible has supplied key theological arguments in favor of slavery ("the curse of Ham"), which it abundantly legislates, along with the resounding impetus for the revolt and emancipation of slaves and other liberation movements (the Exodus).[33]

In this general context, which is hardly about some return to a primordial past (the Bible is not past but a persistent and enduring resource and even engine of thought, language, practices), what I want to address by way of Hagar and Sarah is "a form of relationality, a set of practices, a form of labor, [and] an embodied experience," rather than symbols.[34] I register the neglected relevance of these two figures with regard to both motherhood and slavery as political problems, and of the portentous framing provided by Paul's reading of the biblical text, which was, moreover, decisively seconded by Augustine. This is a reading that, no less ubiquitous, once again, for its unrecognizability (astonishing, really), has articulated, accompanied, and intensified a fraught constellation and a recurring story, a long history of motherhood and slavery, later of slavery and race as well. Here is the difficulty and the ambiguity of the matter that, conveyed for centuries by a resilient lexicon, has structured and even governed, politically, therefore, both motherhood and slavery, ultimately slavery and race. For in the Bible, and at least since Paul, Hagar—that "shadow," as the famously mother-loving Augustine described her, "the foreshadowing symbol [that] was itself foreshadowed"—is undoubtedly considered a slave, a servant and a slave.[35] Since Paul, the dialectic of mother and slave—a tale of two cities—imprinted itself, at times with extreme violence, at times in extreme silence, on a number of traditions, on a number of constitutions (Hagar, it might be recalled, remains unnamed in the Qur'ān, although she is traditionally referred to as "Ishmael's mother").[36] Erich Auerbach, who famously attended to Isaac but not to Ishmael, would have spoken here of *figuration*, of Hagar as a prefiguration of ancient and modern slavery; as a vector of a fraught and peculiar relationship between Christianity and slavery—and, ever popular, freedom—and between Christianity and its others.[37] Tikva Frymer-Kensky refers to Hagar as "the archetype."[38] Hagar certainly, if perhaps ironically, "serves as a model for later Israelite history. As an Egyptian slave, she foreshadows the period of Israel's own slavery in Egypt, and God's intervention on behalf of Hagar and Ishmael similarly foreshadows his later intervention in rescuing Israel from Egypt."[39] Hagar has a longer history, and it stretches to our own days.

Rather than relegating Hagar and Sarah to the realm of some symbolic past, therefore, I want to linger with the attendant significance and enduring resonance of Hagar, powerfully marked and remarked in the African American tradition where "the striking similarities between Hagar's story and African-American's women's history in North America" have been read and experienced.[40] There, they have been eloquently mobilized and commented upon by primarily womanist theologians, but also by other writers and scholars, all of whom have taught me much.[41] What I would like to do in the pages that follow is to reflect on "the *longue durée* of slavery," one that, going back to Paul and Augustine, includes and exceeds as well as prefigures and enables, one that *accompanies* the "American grammar book" (along with the grammar book of other polities, maternal polities) so powerfully theorized and illuminated by Hortense Spillers.[42] After all, Spillers's formulation does quite precisely fit what Saint Paul does, what "our mother Saint Paul" does, since here too, here and henceforth, "motherhood as female bloodrite is outraged, is denied, at the *very same time* that it becomes the

founding term of a human and social enactment."[43] It has long
been the case, in other words, that, figuratively at least, the
enslaved mother, the servant or the nurse, is not considered a
mother, not even an othermother.[44] Whether she was slave or servant, woman or sister, Paul's Hagar is, after all, not called
mother. What then of the relation between, what of the dialectic of, mother and slave?

Before turning more directly to the biblical Hagar, I want to
underscore something else that Spillers illuminates about the
violence inherent to the dialectic between mother and slave. For
the negation and eradication of, coeval with the use and exploitation of maternal functions from, enslaved bodies are one reason
why, Spillers says, "one treads dangerous ground in suggesting an
equation between female gender and mothering." In fact, Spillers
continues, "feminist inquiry/praxis and the actual day-to-day living of numberless American women—black and white—have gone
far to break the enthrallment of a female subject-position to the
theoretical and actual situation of maternity."[45] This is a crucial
insight that, to say it again, is guiding me throughout. For the slave
is granted *neither gender nor maternality.* Slavery, *the slavery of the
enslaved mother,* interrupts motherhood, which is to say that it
breaks the bond between mother and child (sometimes by substituting another child, the child of another, sometimes by
confining the slave to the domination of a sovereign mother). It
also brings about the suspension, even the cessation, of the equation between woman and mother, an equation that was, after
all, enforced and to which women were themselves subjected.
Slavery violently reveals that women are not always mothers,
indeed, that *mothers* are not necessarily mothers, and that the

gender of the mother is never granted. If the slave is not a mother (if the mother is a slave), on the other hand, if she is not a woman, it is because of "the indistinctness of the conditions of 'mother' and 'enslavement'"—the terms are substitutable, all-too interchangeable, but not identical, nor equivalent, and, once again, not granted.[46]

Mother and slave, then. Since just like womanhood and motherhood (the latter being dependent on the former and vice versa) maternality and slavery may be seen, and with good reason, as indissociable. Such has been "the 'nexus' between slavery and surrogacy, between slavery and reproductive technology."[47] Yet the bond is obviously not unbreakable, and things are certainly not simply or always so.[48] Motherhood may be denied, it has been denied, even when, as in the case of Hagar, any and all maternal functions are fulfilled and performed. Accordingly, anyone, any gender, can—freely or, more often, not—*serve* any and (almost) all maternal functions. Men, indeed, fathers, can also mother (according to Isaac Balbus, they should in fact do so).[49] But is service or servitude a maternal function? A maternal dimension? A condition of motherhood? "A woman's work is still too often a kind of slavery," writes Simone de Beauvoir in her chapter on mothers.[50] She may have meant: a *mother's* work. Vicky Shiran makes the argument sharper. "The moment a woman becomes a mother is a wonderful and graced moment," she writes. It is also a most "cruel operation she performs toward herself: she pierces her ear [as the biblical slaves renouncing manumission] out of her own will in order to be remade into a servant [or slave, *shifhah*] to her loved ones, and entirely helpless with regard to the love and compassion that flood her, she subjects her

own life to the needs of her children till death undoes her."[51] Some
maternal functions demand service and even a kind of servitude,
which certainly does not make "mother" a simple synonym of
"slave." Nor does it make "mother" a female verb. It is sadly common that, between two individuals, say, "an unequal complemen-
tarity" is established "in which one person plays master, the other
slave," and particularly so under persistent gender arrangements.[52] Under persistent *maternal* arrangements. Such possibili-
ties implicate mothers and are all too often actualized in and upon
women first of all. And it may be that, as Jessica Benjamin has
argued, "the groundwork for this division is laid in the mother's
renunciation of her own will, in her consequent lack of subjectivity for her children."[53] Or else, the division of maternal labor, and
the dialectic of mother and slave, remains to be acknowledged and
thought. For mothers must be mothered. And, as indisputable as
the fact that mothers are, for the most part, women (which is why
I continue to refer to mothers in the feminine), there are slaves
who have been denied their maternality, even as they have been
mothers or mothering. The hierarchical division (or divisions),
indeed, the heterogeneous separation between the terms (woman,
slave, mother) is as essential to maintain in all cases, as is their
co-implications. Maternal roles and functions are not, nor
should they be, restricted to women, attributed exclusively to
them, *and* they can be denied, dangerously and violently denied,
of the very (mostly female) bodies that perform them. They partake of hierarchical divisions that are and can be mobilized,
actualized, and negated too. That mothers are not all women
may thus be described, biblically enough, as a blessing and a
curse. It is a *cause célèbre* of many feminists, queer and trans

thinkers and activists, and it is also a theoretical and practical, technological and medical, which is also to say, economic, possibility that has enabled the denial of motherhood (for slaves, among other devastating historical instances, and for others, other mothers). Such possibility has been actualized for longer than we often realize in the concrete figures of slaves, nurses, and wet nurses, of servants and nannies, and of many other othermothers. It is not likely to decrease within current economic and geopolitical arrangements, not with "artificial wombs" or other medical "advances."

HEGEL IN CANAAN

So what of slavery? What of service and servitude? It does not take much effort to recognize in Hagar a function, a number of sedimented functions. Let us condense them, for now, as mother and slave.[54] Hagar figures as an artificial womb, a legal and technological extension of Sarah, an instrument writ large, and indeed a slave.[55] If Hagar is an image (image of an image, wrote Augustine). She is undoubtedly an image of what Zakiyyah Iman Jackson calls "the black mater(nal)," those "discursive-material trace effects and foreclosures of the dialectic," not just of "hegemonic common sense," but of a long history and structure, which must contend with the "nullification of black maternity."[56]

In Genesis 16, Hagar is emphatically not a mother, nor is she meant to be or become one. Sarah (still called Saraï at this point) turns to Abram (not yet Abraham) and appeals to him: "You see that the Lord has prevented me from bearing children; go in to my slave; it may be that I shall obtain children, *ibbāneh,* by her."[57] As many have remarked, Sarah is making a legal claim, which defines the situation she initiates by right and defines the role of her slave in it: just as the (unnamed) slave is her property, so the child will be hers. She, Sarah, is and will be the mother. Which is why the text makes explicit that it is Sarah (and not Abraham) who "took Hagar the Egyptian, her slave," just as it is Sarah who "gave her," who gave Hagar "to her husband Abram as a wife." Here might be the place to recall that Hagar the Egyptian has long been understood as being of noble lineage, a daughter of Pharaoh, the later believed to have given her away.[58] In convoluted ways, within herself and in an odd (and, provisionally, partial) mirroring of Sarah, Hagar is a slave and a mother, a queen and an exile.[59]

Before Hegel, Hagar afforded us the opportunity to "deepen our understanding of the slave's work not only as forced labor but also as the psychic work of grappling with internalized forms of oppression."[60] Hagar looks at Sarah. Her "pregnancy-gaze," as Ruth Tsoffar explains, signals that the two women "enter into an intersubjective exchange of looks and power."[61] In that exchange, in the uneven distribution, the uneven confrontation, of life and death, the servant or slave becomes. She becomes "a consciousness that is *forced back* into itself."[62] Which is to say that it is here the slave (or servant, depending on your translation) that "will take the inward turn and convert itself into true self-sufficiency."[63] It makes sense, therefore, that when Hagar "saw that she had conceived," she came to understand her situation, herself, otherwise. Thus, "in the way that mastery showed that its essence is the inversion of what mastery wants to be, so too in its consummation will servitude become the opposite of what it immediately is." Having become that which Sarah wanted to have and be ("Sarai said to Abram, 'May the wrong done to me be on you! I gave my slave to your embrace, and when she saw that she had conceived, she looked on me with contempt'"), Hagar is forced back onto herself, brought back to herself. She is, after all, the one who has conceived, not Sarah (Sarah is therefore "no longer in possession of herself," explains Fethi Benslama, she is "no longer sovereign").[64] In a modern translation, we might say that Hagar understands that she is to *mother* Sarah; she is to mother for and instead of Sarah. Consequently, Hagar "looked with contempt on her mistress." No wonder Abraham advises Sarah to put what Hegel calls "the fear of death, the absolute master" in Hagar. "Abram said to Sarai, 'Your slave is in your power; do to her as you please.' Then Sarai dealt harshly with her, and she ran away from her."

What happens at this juncture seems to me to have eluded the attention it deserves. Recall that Paul did grant that Hagar bore children, but he does not call her mother. Paul was not entirely wrong, we saw. His reading of the text simply repeats that, legally, and up to a certain point, Hagar is not a mother. She is no more than an instrument and a surrogate. Hagar is a slave who carries a child that is not hers, nor is the child meant to be hers. Which is why it is crucial to consider that, by the time she compels Hagar to run away to the wilderness, Sarah is doing more than endangering Hagar's life and the life of the unborn child. Sarah is sovereign. She is enacting sovereign power, performing sovereignty's double, lethal gesture. In a way that becomes even more explicit in Genesis 21, Sarah is *exposing* the child, *her* child.

She is willfully and knowingly casting it out, renouncing him as her offspring. Later, in any case, by the time Isaac is born, Sarah looks at that child, at that first child, the one she had asked for, the son that she wanted for herself, the son that was hers and supposed to be hers, and what she sees is not her own child, not her child any longer, but rather "the son of Hagar the Egyptian, whom she had borne to Abraham, playing with her son Isaac." Ishmael, whom God saves twice from the perils of the wilderness (just as he will save Isaac), has now become Hagar's son. But if Ishmael (who at that juncture had not yet been named and whom God himself will name, though the text also gives Abraham the credit), if that child was clearly and legally intended to be Sarah's child, if he remains legally for her to do with as she pleases, as she sovereignly pleases (including, *souveraineté oblige*, killing him), if that child has become exclusively "the son of Hagar the Egyptian," it means that Sarah, whose name means "to rule and to govern," has performed yet another sovereign gesture.[65] She not only exposed the child but also *made Hagar, made the slave, a mother.* From slavery and surrogacy (if not quite out of it), for the better and for the worse, "Hagar is no longer simply a womb at the service of her masters's posterity."[66] She has now moved and entered a new status: motherhood. Delores Williams is therefore correct when she argues that, upon leaving, Hagar is also depriving Sarah of her motherhood. From being a slave, Hagar has now become a mother (the mother Sarah had become and is now no longer). More precisely, *as a slave still, she is now also a mother.* This, then, is the dialectic of mother and slave. "The angel of the Lord found her by a spring of water in the wilderness, the spring on the way to Shur. And he said, 'Hagar, slave of Sarai, where have you come from and where are you going?' She said, 'I am running away from my mistress Sarai.' The angel of the Lord said to her, 'Return to your mistress, and submit to her'" (Genesis 16).

It is evident that Hagar remains a slave. She is mother and slave, encompassing, if not sublating, the movement of her (and Sarah's) becoming. Hagar is and remains Sarah's slave, and Sarah is and remains her mistress. This is the story and history, the trajectory and historicity, of Hagar. This is where Hagar comes from and where she is going, where she returns and must return. Having said that, Hagar is also the subject of an annunciation (as Abraham was, as other mothers would be), the subject of prophecy and of revelation. She is divinely told that she is a mother, that she is, indeed, a founding mother, a figure less of birth than of futurity, the continued existence, the reproduction, of a collective. In time. "The angel of the Lord also said to her, 'I will so greatly multiply your offspring that they cannot be counted for multitude.' And the angel of the Lord said to her, 'Now you have conceived and shall bear a son; you shall call him Ishmael, for the Lord has given heed to your affliction'" (Genesis 16).

At this point, Hagar is both mother and slave (as well as prophet and slave, as Savina Teubal, Delores Williams, and, surprisingly, Spinoza, recognized), which certainly demonstrates that the dialectic of mother and slave—in Hegel long interpreted according to these distinct perspectives—is not only an economic, legal, social, or political relation between two individuals, but occurs within an individual (though not unified) self, as it were. There is a double movement here, which Hegel might have better described in the feminine. For, between Hagar and Sarah, "each sees *the other* do the same as *she* does; each herself does what she demands of the other and for that reason also does what she does *only* insofar as the other does the same."[67] Yet, Hagar can just as well be represented "as the doing of one self-consciousness," as one mother, at any rate, who can (and perhaps must) occupy the two positions at once.[68] Mother and slave. Or as Hegel puts it, "the truth of the self-sufficient consciousness is thus the servile consciousness."[69] Incidentally, this is the second time the text tells us Hagar is pregnant, something the rabbis understood as a double pregnancy. As if reproduction necessitated its own proliferation.

Subsequently, Hagar, who will soon become an Abrahamic figure, saved by an angel of the Lord, and whose child will be rescued, just as Isaac was, by divine intervention; Hagar, who is already singular among women in being the addressee of a divine revelation and of a divine promise; Hagar, the mother, also performs that most significant of maternal, I mean, biblical gestures. Hagar engages in naming. Just as Adam had and Eve too, mother of us all, who, somehow brazenly, named Cain, Hagar here names not a child, but God himself. "So she named the Lord who spoke to her, 'You are El-roi,' for she said, 'Have I really seen God and remained alive after seeing him?' Therefore the well was called Beer-lahai-roi; it lies between Kadesh and Bered. Hagar bore Abram a son, and Abram named his son, whom Hagar bore, Ishmael. Abram was eighty-six years old when Hagar bore him Ishmael" (Genesis 16).

Aside from confirming that Hagar is a prophetess, a mother-prophetess who has seen and named God, the text also reiterates that Ishmael is her child.[70] He is also Abraham's child, of course. Is he no longer Sarah's child? Recall that Hagar is still Sarah's property. She is still Sarah's slave, and Sarah is still her mistress. Is Sarah a mother?

In the final act of this story, Sarah—now and again a mother herself—renounces Hagar as her property. The mother casts the othermother out, she casts the slave out into exile and toward death. Sarah does so for the second time, saying to Abraham, "Cast out this slave woman [gareš ha-amah ha-zot] with her son, for the son of this slave woman shall not inherit along with my son Isaac" (Genesis 21:10). As I have already said, Sarah, a discriminating mother in all the senses of that term, and a sovereign to boot, is clearly exposing the child, her first child, and thereby confirming or, rather, establishing and instituting (albeit after God has already done so) "the broken and irreducible maternity" of Hagar.[71] Consider that the text no longer refers to Hagar as shifḥah but as amah, a term that may or may not be related to, but certainly resonates with, the word em (or mother), omenet (or nurse), and perhaps amanah (contract).[72] Or indeed to ummah.[73] Wishing to deprive the child of his inheritance, Sarah's intentions are not exactly opaque. Practically speaking, though, she is depriving her younger son Isaac of an obvious maternal presence (and herself of indispensable child care). She is also depriving the older child of the conditions of his survival. And the mother too. And so, unsurprisingly, mother and child are in mortal danger. They are facing death. It is at this point that Hagar, mother that she is, assumes, in her turn, the same yet another maternal function, a sovereign function. Hagar too leaves the child—perhaps no longer quite *her* child therefore, as the text suggests—to die, actively casting him out, unmothering him. "When the water in the skin was gone, she cast the child [*vatišlaḥ et ha-yeled*] under one of the bushes. Then she went and sat down opposite him a good way off, about the distance of a bowshot, for she said, 'Do not let me look on the death of the child.' And as she sat opposite him, she lifted up her voice and wept."

Amaryah Armstrong comments on this passage that "the risk the fugitive poses to sovereignty is also a risk to the self."[74] Armstrong is right, of course. Yet neither Hagar nor Ishmael are going to die, even if they come dangerously close. The angel of the Lord intervenes just as they will for Isaac, and Ishmael will continue to grow, individually and collectively, into a great nation, as promised. Accordingly, Hagar will continue to accompany him as his mother, finding him a wife among her people, the Egyptians. Some rabbis further contend that she ultimately returns to Abraham, redeemed and bearing the name Keturah, after Sarah's death. Sovereignty at risk. Is there any other kind? In the dialectic of mother and slave, Hagar would thus become the mistress as well.[75]

It takes a village to raise a child. It takes at least two mothers. You may argue that it takes one mother who is two, at once mother and slave. A plurality of maternal functions, in any case, among which service and servitude cannot be glossed over, for therein lies a truth—partial as it might be—of motherhood, of a mother's work, of the work of mothers. Ishmael, in any case, is the child of two mothers. Recall that in a text that has God command *both* animals and humans to "be fruitful and multiply" it is impossible to distinguish absolutely between what we might call, in an idiom that could not be more foreign to the Bible, nature and law, *physis* and *nomos*.[76] Sarah remains Ishmael's mother. That is to say, she becomes Ishmael's mother, his first mother. Her becoming-mother, a privilege she exercises in her sovereign capacity as mistress and slave-owner, is dependent on her using and abusing the slave she treats as an instrument, a physiological and technological extension of herself. At first, then, Hagar is, what we would call, a surrogate, but not—not quite or not yet—a surrogate *mother*. A slave indeed, as many have argued, and for sound socioeconomic and geopolitical reasons that have, with a little help from Paul and Augustine, scandal-ously long weighed on and defined the color line.[77] Yet, by Sar-ah's sovereign actions, and by God's too, Hagar also becomes a mother. She is Ishmael's second mother (and the last shall be first, as Frantz Fanon knew), making him the first child, the first biblical child of two mothers. Is there, here too, an other kind? Isaac, at any rate, will soon follow, raised by both mothers too, until Hagar's final exit, her final exile, that is.[78] Ishmael and Isaac are hardly the last, as we shall soon see, hardly the last to visibly signal toward two mothers. Two mothers, in any case, two moth-ers for now: the mother and the slave.[79] For the mother is indeed more than a "faceless mirror, altruistic servant, or otherwise slave to the child."[80] The mother is more than that, yes, but is she not also that, also a servant or slave to the child?[81] Who is the sov-ereign here, who the slave? It is from Sarah and Hagar that we learn this harsh, and perhaps undecidable, lesson in subjection, though as I suggested, Hagar alone—that is, Hagar herself inso-far as she is always two, both mother and slave—conveyed that very lesson already, that very truth. "The difference of the slave-mother is both marked and disappeared."[82] She is the same and another mother, split between two poles, two functions, of the maternal.[83] I might have called that lesson, after Freud, "The Mother Hagar and the Monotheistic Religion." It is a lesson, we shall see, of yet unheard proportions.[84]

Chapter Two

OF MOTHERS BORN

IT TAKES A VILLAGE to raise a child.

In the previous chapter, I proposed that we linger and reflect upon that village, upon the polity that, in my argument, must and does *mother* mothers (however badly or poorly). Over the course of this book, let me repeat, I am interested in thinking the political otherwise than as paternal or patriarchal, otherwise than fraternal. In ways we have yet to understand, the political must rather be acknowledged as *maternal*.

In the introduction, I began to speak about my mother and, more generally, about the way she has inscribed herself upon me. I spoke about the writing of mothers. The claim I begun to advance is that motherhood is a form of writing in the world. Thinking of writing, with the (discrete) help of Derrida, enables a questioning, perhaps a mapping, of *the maternal field*, the expanse and the limits within which mothers inscribe themselves. Writing, maternal writing, begins to render explicit a list or series of maternal functions, beyond birth and care, of which there are many. I then went on to offer a close reading of *two* maternal functions, of the two maternal figures that are, in the Bible, Hagar and Sarah. Invoking Hegel's famous confrontation, I referred to the dialectic of mother and slave. I did so inspired by James Baldwin (who proposes that Blacks occupy a maternal position and maternal function vis-à-vis whites) and by way of Saint Paul (who demonstrates, in Hortense Spillers's terms, that "motherhood as female bloodrite is outraged, is denied, at the very same time that it becomes the founding term of a human and social enactment"). I concluded by recalling that there is a prejudice that goes deeper than the belief in the one God of monotheism, namely, the belief in the uniqueness and unicity of the mother. With the dialectic of mother and slave, with Hagar and Sarah, I began to underscore the two mothers, the division and duality of mothers. "A mother's body is a crowded space, like the community of Naples . . ." like other cities and collectives.[1]

■ ■ ■

It takes a village to raise a child.

But what does it take to raise a mother? To become one? Just as the social contract begins with fully grown (white) men, most books about motherhood set about with an all-too-obvious beginning, with pregnancy and birth. Accordingly, medical textbooks, psychological manuals and psychoanalytic treatises often insist on identifying the mother as "the matter of origins,"[2] locating the mother almost exclusively in the earliest, prelinguistic stages of the infant, the very beginnings of the infant's development.[3] Jennifer Nash points out that feminism too has made and "remade birthing" along with "the idea that birth is understood as a self-making event," a privileged and unique "experience . . . that marks the transition to motherhood."[4] Making and remaking divides this event, however, and suggests a proliferation. Indeed, even if new and singular, motherhood and maternality (the latter word seems more fitting than Hannah Arendt's "natality") cannot be reduced to the event of birth or to new beginnings and must therefore be distinguished from them.[5] Motherhood is rather repetition—the lengthy work of repetition. This is no reduction but the very necessity of the matter.[6] As Honaida Ghanem explains, motherhood "involves the execution of certain ceremonies, behaviors, declarations, physical functions, and verbal patterns that are constantly recycled and on occasion emphasized."[7] More precisely, perhaps, motherhood is iteration, the unavoidable writing and rewriting of many marks and stages, phases and chapters, the manifest or latent returns of mothers past and of their marks.[8] "Every natural mother is already a substitute," is the way Luisa Muraro strikingly puts it.[9] This applies to each and every mother. When I insist that no mother is one, this is also what I mean. Nor is any mother born one. Or "we could say that a mother is the set of all possible sets, the one all-embracing set that contains everything, including itself."[10] As we have already seen, out of many, one must become a mother, repeat (and thus divide) oneself into and onto mothers. Accordingly, words like *generation* or *reproduction*—of the family, of the nation, of the species —words like *mother* signal the iterability, rather than the unity or unicity, of maternality.[11]

THE MOTHER'S TWO BODIES

But the mothering of mothers, the proliferation of mothers, which we have begun to register, to count and to recount, itself begins—without beginning—at two. This is not some magic number. In the history of algebra before the invention of zero, one was not a number, for numbers can only exist once you begin to count, which is to say, at the number two. Two is a beginning that is not a beginning. It is the minimal number of parties in a contract, in this instance, the maternal contract to which I shall return. In some cases, two might also refer to "two psychic sites of intense maternal deprivation."[12] It is, at any rate, the sign and the number of repetition, the minimal way of signifying that, if "there is no such thing as a baby," as Winnicott famously had it, there is never, *pace* Winnicott, only one mother either, no mother who is ever one. Only a prejudice that is, if not older, certainly stronger than monotheism, could ever convince us otherwise. Queer theorist Shelley Park called that prejudice "monomaternalism," and there is every reason to follow her in adopting the term, if only to mark our "inability to name and grammaticalize the mother."[13] Which is to say, to count the mothers. And before we replace or supplement *mother* with alternative terms like *othermothers* (as Patricia Hill Collins has advocated) or *alloparents* (as Sarah Blaffer Hrdy has proposed), or else a more general *parenting*—however necessary it might be, we will have to linger with the duality of mothers and with a different nuclear family, different nuclear families, which, though canonical by every possible standard, have failed to draw the attention they deserve. The consequences, we shall see, are remarkable.

We have already encountered what might be aptly summarized as "a splitting or doubling of the maternal function that involves a biological mother and juridical one, or a mother and a 'de facto' mother who does not count, or a mother proper and a nurse or nanny."[14] We have encountered motherhood as experience and motherhood as institution (Rich). We have gotten to know the mother and the slave. We have encountered, in other words, Sarah and Hagar in the Bible and in Paul's Letter to the Galatians and since. Now, I do want to be mindful here of recent criticism regarding the ubiquitous perspective of the Child, a persistent orientation toward the future, which has been all too easily embraced, and particularly with regard to political thought.[15] Still, Ishmael and Isaac both had two mothers, Sarah and Hagar. This "myth," if it is one, cannot be reduced to some dream of matriarchy. It is rather, as Rita Segato says, "a page taken from social history."[16] For Ishmael and Isaac are not the only ones, and the fact that their "case," their maternal case, has attracted so little attention speaks, it seems to me, more than a page. It speaks volumes. It is certainly worth a couple of lectures, perhaps even a small book.

Hagar and Sarah. Two mothers. Such is the shape of what I have begun to call "the maternal contract." It is, at once, a sexual and a racial contract.[17] It is also an economic and political contract.[18] A more accurate contract, it seems, than many have otherwise proposed in order to reflect on the magical passage concisely described by that great theorist of the village, Henry Sumner Maine, the passage "from status to contract." And one might invoke here the *many* arduous and conflicted passages (the mother-work, that is) mediated thereby, and retrospectively figured, as nature and culture, infancy and language, fantasy and reality, body and psyche, affect and reason, private and public, and more. I refer to a contract, to a maternal contract, because it involves two parties at least, two unequal parties (just as the sexual contract and the racial contract, presupposed and buttressed by the social contract), and first of all two mothers.[19] It is also a contract of mother and child, indeed of mothers and children, once again unequal.[20] In any case, we shall see in the next chapter that it is also a revocable contract, which sustains or undoes a collective, the necessary infrastructure of any collective. Given its lack of visibility, it might as aptly be described as a foreclosure. "This is a foreclosure," Segato writes, "a disregard or non-knowledge, of the maternal and the racial at once, of blackness and the mother."[21] In starker terms, "slavery and motherhood."[22] This is not a stereotype, a mere historical chapter (however momentous), nor is it some Kleinian simplification. It is the structure and the history of the maternal, of mothering and of child care, of child adoption, and of education in their transnational and economic dimensions, all of which have long been "infiltrated by a form of raciality," just as "raciality is infiltrated by motherhood."[23] Call it, as I propose to do after Ernst Kantorowicz, "the mother's two bodies."[24]

Hagar and Sarah. The Hebrew, the Egyptian. And, as if Paul's resonant echoing of the two mothers (but which is the mother here, which the slave?) was not spectacular enough, we recall what we already knew, which—but is it fair to single him out?—Sigmund Freud, no less spectacularly, ignored. For Moses too had two mothers. One Hebrew, one Egyptian. All according to that most recurring of structures, the mother and the slave, the legal and the biological, the mother and the wet nurse. Now, I say that Freud ignored it, but I only mean by this that, expert as he was on that *fort/da* game, Freud did not comment upon mothers, upon Moses's mothers, in *Moses and Monotheism*.[25] Freud, who, like Gilles Deleuze after him, elsewhere counted up to three ("the three forms taken by the figure of the mother in the course of a man's life"), did enjoy telling the following Jewish joke.[26] "The boy Itzig is asked in grammar school, 'Who was Moses?' and answers, 'Moses was the son of an Egyptian princess.' 'That's not true,' says the teacher. 'Moses was the son of a Hebrew mother. The Egyptian princess found the baby in a casket.' But Itzig answers: 'Says she!' "[27]

The Hebrew, the Egyptian. There is no stronger evidence of the prejudice that monomaternalism constitutes than this: there can only be one mother. From Eve and Mary to Winnicott and Bowlby, the notion has been so often displayed and reiterated, preceding and buttressing the modern myth of the individual, it should have aroused more suspicion.[28] Indeed, I find it amazing, to give another example, that Adrienne Rich herself waits until the penultimate chapter, that is, until the end of her penultimate chapter, in *Of Woman Born,* before mentioning the fact that she too had two mothers. "As a child raised in what was essentially the South, Baltimore in the segregated 1930s, I had from birth not only a white, but a Black mother"[29] Rich does not refer to Sarah and Hagar, but she knows she was not the only one. Not unlike Segato, Rich particularizes and restricts the reach of her knowledge and acknowledges no more than the singularity of a particular time and place, as the very limit of dual maternality or, one might say, of the maternal field.[30] The phenomenon, the structure, of a double or divided maternality, is in fact widespread.[31] In fairy tales, most notably, where one recalls the figure of the stepmother, that always vilified othermother.[32] It is also what Marxist feminism has attended to, to a significant extent.[33] "She *was* a mother," insists Rich—as if to convince herself. "My Black mother was 'mine.'"[34]

It is at any rate obvious that the dialectic of mother and slave, the mother and the nurse, wet nurse or nanny (grandmother or stepmother, aunt or sister), which is to say, as well, the very material, political economy of motherhood, has been recurring in the—shall we call it collective?—unconscious for some time now.[35] Call it a repression, "a double Abrahamic repression."[36] For it is certainly the case that "having two mothers and two lineages doesn't conform to the Ten Commandments. God says, 'Honor thy father and thy mother,' not 'thy mothers.'"[37] But what are we to make of the mothers of the twelve tribes of Israel, mothers and slaves, who together and unequally, just as the four matriarchs (but *sans* Hagar) accompany the children of Israel as they merge or emerge into a people. And what are we to make of Moses's two mothers? What of the long history—as long as history itself—of midwives, wet nurses, slaves, stepmothers, and witches?[38]

At a more recent end, what of the "Czech Catholic nanny, the *Kinderfrau* who cared for [Freud] for the first two and a half years of his life" and "abruptly disappeared?" Freud's nurse and servant was his own "second mother."[39] This is the same Freud who, we know, was particularly fond of Leonardo da Vinci; the same Freud, who wrote about Leonardo that "he had had two mothers." Sarah Kofman, who would later poignantly narrate her own tragic childhood between two mothers, revisits Freud on da Vinci and explains that "since Leonardo had had, so to speak, two mothers, he gave two mothers to Jesus. The peculiarity of the position of the two women [in the *Virgin and Child with St Anne* painting] . . . expresses the peculiarity of the life of Leonardo, who was raised by his mother and by his step-mother, who was younger than the mother."[40] One might have to be capable of rendering no less than a Solomonic judgment, therefore, in order to discern one mother from the other, one good mother from a bad one (an Egyptian vulture, say, in Leonardo's case, according to Freud), or to adjudicate between mother and nurse, mother and slave.[41] Before attempting to do so, to render some form of maternal justice from Moses to Freud and beyond, I cannot resist mentioning that, according to a medieval midrash, not only Moses but David too, that is to say, King David himself, was "the son of two mothers: Jesse's wife and Jesse's maidservant."[42] And the prophet of Islam too is said to have called two women "mother."

I might have stopped here or elsewhere in my count, and I would have, I think, had I not learned that there is more still to consider. Hardly a minor character, the Buddha also "figures in Buddhist literature not only as a perfectly awakened buddha, but also as the adored son of two different mothers."[43] This fact too "has never adequately been considered before, nor has the relationship between [the two mothers, incidentally, two sisters married to the same king] been explored at any length."[44] Indeed, "existing scholarship" on the two mothers, Māyā and Mahāprajāpatī, "has consistently failed to consider these two figures in relation to each other,"[45] For our part, we might follow a different distribution of maternal functions, the distinction between the two mothers, between "a mother who dies and a mother who survives."[46] Māyā is an "idealized birth-giver," perfect in every way and, because she dies (within seven days), untouched by the impurities of this world.[47] The other mother, on the other hand, her sister Mahāprajāpati, is the nursing and caring, nourishing and sustaining mother, the toiling mother, whose labor and work is also a work of mourning. She is "the mother who grieves over her son's departure" (91; though Māyā too is described as eternally grieving). Manifestly a political figure, Mahāprajāpati is also "the leader of a large assembly" and an institution-builder in this world. She is the founder of the first order of Buddhist nuns.

Here is not the place to engage further a Buddhist tradition I am insufficiently familiar with, except perhaps to point out two things. First, that this tradition also formulated a complex ideal that "encouraged" idealized sons ("the ideal monk, the perfect arhat, or the male bodhisattva") "to cultivate emotions and attitudes that in some way militate *against* the particularity of the mother-son bond—either by encouraging the son to recognize *no mother* or by encouraging the son to recognize *many mothers*."[48] The second thing follows from the first, for "the concept of 'motherhood' seems to be broadened, such that a mother's 'mothering' can extend to those besides her own children (without compromising her special love for them), while those who are not mothers themselves can 'mother' society at large."[49] Two mothers, to begin with. Two mothers instead of a beginning. Two mothers because mothers must be mothered. As the medieval *Sefer Hasidim* recommends to all, "you should consider all the people of Israel your own children and tend to all their needs."[50]

As I have already intimated, the list of dual mothers is longer still. I will just mention in passing that Socrates, who may have had two wives, also finds himself between two mothers, two maternal figures, at the very least. First, Socrates' own mother, the midwife Phaenarete, and then Diotima, who famously teaches him that "all of us are pregnant, Socrates, both in body and in soul, and, as soon as we come to a certain age, we naturally desire to give birth." But rather than linger with the disputes that surround Plato's words—beginning with the word *khōra*—I shall turn to another major figure of Greek antiquity, a figure whose mothers, whose two mothers, have also failed to attract significant attention.

HAMLET OR HECUBA

Among all the sons, all the once young princes, I have reviewed and attended to (Ishmael and Isaac, Moses, David, Solomon, Buddha, and Socrates), none have had their familial, nay, maternal history more exposed—and *exposed* is definitely the right word here—than the one I have kept here for last, namely, Oedipus. For Oedipus surely had two mothers. Who does not know this? What is most astonishing, though, is how little significance the fact of his dual motherhood seems to have had toward an interpretation of the play or, indeed, toward a consideration of maternality and motherhood.

But before I turn to these mothers, to Oedipus's mothers, I want to explain the title of this section, which I borrow from famous German jurist Carl Schmitt's reading of *Hamlet*. There,

Schmitt himself insists on attending to the titles of the works he reads ("It is called 'Hamlet in Wittenberg' without being equal to the powerful theme that is evoked by such a title" he writes), but he does not reflect on his own, which posits a remarkable, indeed powerful, alternative.[51] Hamlet or Hecuba: His Majesty the Baby or else, the mother.[52] Reading *Hamlet,* that modern replay of Oedipus, from the perspective of the mother—or is it mothers? Hecuba is after all, and literally, mother *and* slave—is quite clearly what Schmitt advocates ("Hamlet stands as a kind of watershed, subjecting to maternal presence the relationships previously exempted from that presence," confirms Janet Adelman).[53] Along with a few famous readers (T. S. Eliot, Jacques Lacan, and Adelman among them), Schmitt sees the mother, the queen mother, as central to the play.[54] For Schmitt, more precisely, the question is that of Gertrude's guilt. Schmitt says so, however, without identifying her crime, which, one would think, is at least double. Double: just as a queen who is also a mother might be, a mother who is a slave. The queen's two bodies. That Gertrude is conflated with Ophelia and, moreover, marked by the memory of grieving mothers—mothers like Hecuba or Niobe (the very same Niobe, incidentally, that Walter Benjamin offered as the paradigmatic victim of mythical violence)—only adds to her complexity or, perhaps, to her duality.[55] For if Gertrude is guilty, it is of both matricide and regicide (Schmitt later mentions tyrannicide). And perhaps of infanticide as well (Adelman explains that Gertrude does subject her son "to her annihilating power").[56] It is here, at any rate, in the mother's (and the queen's) real or fantasized "power to annihilate," that we might recognize "the centrality of Gertrude: for the play localizes its pervasive boundary panic in Hamlet's relationship with his mother."[57] Hamlet—who does call Claudius "mother" ("Mother. Father and mother is man and wife, man and wife is one flesh; so mother") and even "dear mother" —is caught between the queen as a political being and his mother as a sexual being, along with the strange imperative to spare her ("Nor let thine soul contrive against thine mother aught," says the Ghost).[58] We might say that Hamlet is also caught between a mother he has lost, a lost or absent mother, and an "all-too alive mother."[59] Either way, "the Queen, the Queen's to blame."[60] To add—or subtract—to the injury, "in her last moments, [Gertrude] seems to become a wonderfully homey presence for her son, newly available to him as the loving and protective mother of childhood, worrying about his condition, wiping his face as he fights, even perhaps intentionally drinking the poison intended for him."[61] A new mother. A second mother. No longer "the annihilating mother" but "an internal good mother."

Where to begin, then? The mother or "His Majesty the Baby?"[62] Carl Jung did contribute by agreeing that the mother might have been important. But he only recognized her in and as the monster.[63] "If only Oedipus had been sufficiently intimidated by the frightening appearance of the 'terrible' or 'devouring' Mother whom the Sphinx personified!"[64] Yet, for the duration of the play, and until the final revelation, Oedipus knows himself to have one mother (*not* a monster), and one mother only. Do we remember her name? Can we say her name? She is, we later learn, his adoptive mother and also the queen of Corinth. And though, never having become a "feminist archetype" of any decade, her name is mostly forgotten (even if the tradition grants her, in fact, two names: Merope, mentioned by Sophocles, and Periboea), we ourselves do well to recall her, to recall that she is the one who does all the work of raising Oedipus.[65] It is she, to begin with, who names the wounded child we all know as Oedipus (not unlike Moses, who was named by Pharaoh's daughter, the mother who raised him). Jocasta did not name, nor could she have named, the child, if only for dramatic reasons (had she known his name, she would have recognized him for who he was). Nor, we can grant, did Laius, who would not have acknowledged and recognized him as his son—in a legal sense—before exposing him.[66] Exposure is, after all, precisely the opposite of a parental claim in this context. Oedipus is rejected. He is neither named, nor known and is never *claimed* by his Theban parents. Oedipus knows who named him, who raised him, but he does not know he was adopted, certainly not that he was saved from murderous parents. Murderous parents? In his journey of "self" discovery, what Oedipus ultimately learns, what he is exposed to, as it were, anew is that it was his "own" mother, which is to say, his recently discovered (other) mother, Jocasta, who "was the instrument of his ghastly fate."[67] It was Jocasta who gave him away to the shepherd in order to kill him ("HERDSMAN The child was called his child; but she within your wife would tell you best how all this was—OEDIPUS She gave it to you?—HERDSMAN Yes she did, my lord.—OEDIPUS To do what with it?—HERDSMAN Make away with it.—OEDIPUS She was so hard—its mother?"). Oedipus was raised by a toiling, and caring, mother whom he believed to be his one and only mother. It is from her, and from his father Polybus of Corinth, that Oedipus flees in order to escape the curse of the oracle. And it is Merope that he confesses to fearing.[68] Yet, with this final revelation, he does not lose a mother but rather gains (and loses too) a second mother, "so hard," and who turns out to have been the "first."

Let us linger with the mothers, then. With Jocasta and with Merope. The two mothers, the two queens, hardly seem to offer a most compelling illustration for my argument that mother and slave constitute the basic structure of motherhood, of motherhood as dual motherhood. Let us ignore that Merope has disappeared into oblivion, that she is not remembered as Oedipus's mother, that the city she rules "was known as a slave center."[69] Let us ignore the fact that Oedipus himself raises the possibility that he himself is, in fact, a slave, the son of *a slave mother*, as he himself repeatedly imagines and dreads ("Keep up your heart, Jocasta. Though I'm proved a slave, thrice slave, and though my mother be thrice slave, you'll not be shown to be of lowly lineage," 1062–63). Let us ignore, finally, that like Hagar, Merope is marked by exile, in fact, a double exile (hers and her son's).

When it comes to audiences, it is clear that, for the better and for the worse, one mother, Jocasta, has been remembered (getting to name a "complex," like her son and husband), whereas the other mother has been almost entirely forgotten, yet another invisible carrier of "our inability to name and grammaticalize the mother."[70] All this would be symptomatic enough to recognize a clear hierarchy, as well as a dependence and a bond, between and among the mothers. The mother, the slave. For the hierarchy finally corresponds to a very clear division of roles and functions, a division of maternal labor, between them, a "split," as Rachel Bowlby writes, "between the nurturing and the rejecting mother," a split that "separates Merope and Jocasta," but also binds them as mothers.[71] To repeat, Merope is not only likely to have named Oedipus herself, she is the one who raised him, the one who toiled and did the work of mothering (you know, like queens do, but bear with me here), the one with whom and close to whom, the one thanks to whom, Oedipus became who he was. Merope loved Oedipus as her son, and she is the one Oedipus loved as a mother, as the queen and sovereign mother she was and remains, the mother he loves and fears, and fears committing incest with.[72] Jocasta, on the other hand, did not care for him, not as a mother, not as a queen mother. In fact, Jocasta did much worse than not care for and protect the child he was. As we already saw, she is explicitly described as having exposed the child, as having given him over to be killed. Jocasta is a killer mother and a killer queen. She is the one who abandons and exposes the child. And before she married that prodigal son upon his return, well before she had their children (to whom she is more than mother, more than one mother, but mother and grand-mother at once), she was already guilty of infanticide. That she did not succeed in that particular endeavor is hardly to her credit—or to that of her husband, King Laius. All the same, we might still want to withdraw all credit and responsibility from her and agree with those who see in Jocasta—and in the complex named after her—a condition "forever contaminated with bond-age . . . a poisonous state of bondage." Mother and slave.[73]

After *Electra*, explains the great French classicist Nicole Loraux, *Oedipus Tyrannus* is "the play of Sophocles where the word 'mother' appears the most."[74] Loraux herself never comments on Merope, although she does underscore that Oedipus imagined himself the son of yet another mother ("Forturne's the mother from whom I spring"), whereas the chorus addresses another other mother,

Mount Cithaeron, as "Oedipus' compatriot, his mother and nurse at once." What Oedipus fails to understand is that one is born from at least two and not only from one (Loraux seems to mean parents, here, as she clings to her own monomaternalism). What he does not know, what "Oedipus does not yet know [is] that Jocasta is double."[75] Loraux gives us a rare and powerful treatment of Jocasta, which provides a crucial illustration, not so much of an alternate beginning (as in, first was "His Majesty the Baby") as of the counting of mothers. Throughout her essay, Loraux in fact insists, as she often does in her work, on duality and division, the duality and division of mother and wife, here, of double mother and double wife.[76] Thus Jocasta is a "double maternal field" or, as the play itself has it, "a field of double sowing."[77] It would be difficult to find a more obvious and manifest example of the duality of mothers than Jocasta "herself," if she is indeed one self.

What I have tried to show, for my part, is that this duality does not stop at Jocasta but unfolds into the dual figure of two mothers, the remembered and the forgotten, the nurturing and the rejecting, the sovereign and the slave. One might pursue this duality and include presence and absence—prior to any father—as well as life and death. Indeed, however we understand the play and the questions it raises, the answers must go through Jocasta, that mother who is mother and wife, mother and grandmother, mother and queen. Jocasta figures a maternal field that, made of divisions, of returns, repetitions, and reiterations, endures and persists, a field that governs the entirety of the plot. The maternal field is a field of inscriptions, indeed, as the metaphor of sowing returns again and again. Jocasta is the space upon which the imprint of the father is found, as paternal legitimacy has no other field of inscription than the field of the mother.[78] And Jocasta too leaves an imprint, as Loraux's title has it. In fact, Jocasta is an imprint, a trace, a writing apparatus. She writes and makes the father and the son, the son king. As Loraux writes, "it is the mother that makes the father [c'est la mère qui fait le père]."[79] Yet, it takes two mothers to make a child, to kill him or keep him, to raise him and to raise him higher still. Merope is hardly diminished in her maternal role, as queen mother, even if her absence from the stage, and from the play's reception, relegates her to a secondary position, the position of the working slave. Be that as it may, prior to "His Majesty the Baby," but also during His "reign," there remains the duality of mothers.

Chapter Three

THE SOVEREIGNTY OF MOTHERS

IT TAKES A VILLAGE to raise a child.

In the previous chapters, I began to write about my mother (I will say more about her in closing) and about the authorial sovereignty of maternal writing. I wrote about the writing of mothers, a writing that has children—and the village, the polity, the world—as its space, as its field of inscription. I sought to map out, to begin to map out that field, that maternal field, as political. I proposed, in other words, to understand the multifarious nature of that village, the village that it takes to become a mother. A village, I have argued, and more generally any collective or polity, is a mother, a plurality of mothers and of maternal functions. It must mother mothers in order to reproduce itself, to preserve and maintain itself in time. My argument, in its most concise formulation, is thus that the political must be thought of as otherwise than paternal or patriarchal; otherwise than fraternal too; rather as maternal.

For multiple reasons, and without restricting myself to a particular period or periodization (Atlantic slavery, modernity), yet learning from and inspired in great part by James Baldwin (who understood Blacks in their maternal position and function vis-à-vis whites) and by Hortense Spillers (who grammaticalized mothers and showed Black mothers caught in the double gesture that exploits and founds, but also denies and even eradicates, motherhood), I have proposed to read the biblical, maternal figures of Hagar and Sarah, the dialectic of mother and slave. I began to identify in the mother and the slave a kind of *Urzelle*, a basic cell of sociality (a "total social fact"), of unequal distribution of maternal functions, a division of maternal labor. This dialectic was also meant to send us on our way toward a questioning of monomaternalism, the deep and enduring prejudice that, stronger than the belief in the one God, identifies one mother and one mother only, the belief, in other words, in the uniqueness and the unicity of the mother. My own count and recount of mothers begins, without beginnings, at two. Hagar and Sarah, Jocasta and Merope, the mother and the slave. Over the course of the chapters thus far, I also tried to evoke, among other maternal functions, a sovereign function, an admittedly still vague concept of maternal sovereignty. In a parallel manner, I also started to sketch something like a "maternal contract." It is to these entangled notions, sovereignty and the maternal contract, that I turn in my final chapter.

■ ■ ■

It takes a village to raise a child.

It requires a contract, an understanding if not a tacit agreement, which itself enables and extends the contract and contact between mother and child.[1] This maternal contract sustains and, in ways we shall explore, *undoes*, the parties involved. It is a crucial, if unacknowledged, condition of possibility for the existence of a collective, of any collective, over time.[2] At stake is the reproduction—the reiteration through time—of that collective, which is to say, the preservation and maintenance of its abiding existence. Over time, then. The reproduction that the maternal contract sustains and enacts is by no means reducible, therefore, to the sexual, to the familial, or to the domestic, although it is obviously related to each of these, perhaps prepares and includes them all. It is not only sexual reproduction that I speak of, even if it has a sexual register (rightly criticized by feminists and by critics of demographic practices). The maternal contract is also (more than) social and (more than) economic. It is racial, and has been for too long, which is to say, that it is locally and globally unequal. It involves and implicates all the members of a collective, all those who have been mothered, and it requires, of necessity, a number of mothers and of maternal functions, whether birthing or aborting, nursing or caring, living or accompanying.[3] Only mothers? For essential and historical reasons, I have foregrounded mothers and slaves. But the maternal contract implicates the polity as a whole, not only its mothers and its slaves, its servants or dependency workers (nannies, nurses, and teachers, "essential workers," you might say, among other maternal roles and functions); and not only the labor force or the cannon fodder of the nation either (rightly targeted by marxists, pacifists and critics of nationalism), and it is therefore collectives at large— and again not only mothers (and daughters), families, or labor forces—who are produced and reproduced under the heading and imperative of reproduction (or of modern demographics, of biopolitics).[4] All collectives that sustain themselves through time are dependent on one form of reproduction or another (and mostly more than one), whether sexual or ritual, social, legal, or economic.[5] And they all need mothers, those who perform and have performed maternal functions.

Maternal functions, and not only birth. For contrary to the obsession carried by a ubiquitous vocabulary of origins or beginnings, of birth and of natality (nature, *natio*, *nasci*), which dominates the political imagination (immigration!), no collective is defined by its foundation alone (no individual either), whether matriarchal or patriarchal, whether mythical or historical.[6] Societies, tribes, classes, or nations are maintained, they are made and transformed, they *reproduce*, by way of repetitions and reiterations through time. Call it, as I have, for paleonymic and historical reasons, for political reasons, the mothering of mothers.[7] Collectives last. They exist and maintain themselves in time rather than merely begin. They do so by way of the number two, at least. Mother and mother, mother and slave, mother and child. Whether they end, what the nature of such end might be—these are questions I do not engage here. I only wish to take the measure of the maternal field. Neither to condone nor advocate its perdurance. As if it were possible.

THE MATERNAL CONTRACT

I have said nothing, throughout this book, about matriarchy. I do not call for some "cult of the Great Mother," or comment on "women who run with the wolves." I do not think, as I have tried to explain, that motherhood is best understood by way of origins, beginnings, or primordial archetypes. I have not, in any case, attempted to write a history of social or political forms, nor to reconstruct their actual or imagined beginnings, archaic, primordial or otherwise. I should nevertheless mention that the formulations proposed by Ifi Amadiume, as she theorized, herself inspired by Cheikh Anta Diop, "African matriarchy," have very much spoken to me ("the *mpuke,* the female mother-focused matricentric unit," for instance, but also "the ideology of *umunne,* the spirit of common motherhood" and the "dialectical relationship between the production unit and relations of production" where "those who eat out of one pot are bound in the spirit of common motherhood...bound as children of a common mother").[8] Late in the writing of this book, I also came across the work of Elva F. Orozco Mendoza, who strikingly proposes to read Mexican social movements that mobilize mothers as formulating a "maternal contract." For Mendoza, who singularly uses the phrase upon which I had chanced, "the mothers' act of coming together in a larger collective body with higher capacity of representation and maneuvre resembles, following the social contract tradition, a subaltern maternal contract."[9] Mothers of the disappeared, Mendoza goes on, make a contract with one another, they come together as a collective body. They also and simultaneously make a pact with their missing offspring. In other words, "they made a pact with their missing children and among themselves."[10] They do so to oppose "differential sovereignty" which divides the political body. Aiming to restore the ties that exist between all members of the polity, "on having institutions that work for all,"[11] the maternal contract seeks to protect otherwise.

It is, therefore, less an alternative to sovereignty, as Mendoza argues, than its condition of possibility.

What I have done, for my part, is to try and describe extended iterations of maternality and motherhood, to read the contract that binds and unbinds two mothers, two mothers at the very least (even if one mother hides another, even if a mother is a dead mother, and even if a mother, any mother, but, for some time now, mostly nonwhite mothers, can always be ignored or denied, abandoned, erased, killed, and, ultimately, forgotten). I underscored the number two (mother and slave) but a more precise, and fuller, description would have to attend to the way the contract binds two and two and two together. The contract is intrinsically and essentially temporal. It always already repeats, in other words, always already proliferates, binding mother and mother on a vertical axis (mother and grandmother), mother and mother on a horizontal axis (mother and slave, nurse or nanny), and binding as well mother and child. The maternal contract is transgenerational—mothers and time—because it cannot be otherwise, because no mother gives birth (only) to herself, nor to a child exclusively her own, in the absence of mothers, in the absence of world; because a mother's imprint is always (on) another mother, and because, like the child of any and every mother, even an unborn one, the mother, any mother, cannot be the only mother.[12] This impossibility does not mean that no mother is ever alone or indeed, abandoned. Yet even then the world around the mother weighs, still, *too* heavily, perhaps mostly by its absence, indifference or worse, it still bears upon her with the most quotidian or extreme demands. All too often, then, mothers are abandoned, unaccompanied, unmothered, but they are never off the hook, never unchained. They are always mothered, if more or less well. All mothers, then, have always already been inscribed as and onto a maternal field and must continue to do so, must continue to mother in the world, with the world (and in the better, if rarer, case, to be mothered by the world), with or without difference.[13] Reproduction, what is often called "social reproduction," is sustained and enabled, rendered possible, by contact and contract, by the maternal contract—the mothering of mothers—which is to say, by tradition and education, languages and rituals, by preservation and also by destruction, as we have begun to consider. The maternal contract is thus ineluctably sexual and racial, intimate and general, economic and political.[14] It is profoundly unequal, therefore, but it is also "continually being rewritten."[15] Like the social contract, *as the social contract*, Zakiyyah Iman Jackson explains, it is "haunted by a sovereignty it theoretically aimed to dethrone but ultimately only appropriates for its Self."[16] Like every contract, like any contact, it can be interrupted. And like all contracts, it can be ended and revoked. Therein lies the sovereignty of mothers.

Now, as Nietzsche well knew (whose own relationship to mothers, and to his mother, deserves more space than I can spend here), we never did away with grammar. Never did away with the distinction of doer and deed, the primacy of doer over deed. More important, we never did away with the "done to," the victim of the deed. But if mother is indeed a verb, we might go back to grammar and to translation. We might go back to reflect on the verb *to kill* not in terms of its "addressee" or victim but in terms of what the deed does to the doer and to God.[17] And I do mean *to kill* and *not to murder* (that translation of the Bible's commandment into "Thou shall not kill" makes nonsense of the ubiquitous distinction, whatever its worth, between killing and murdering, which too many pretend to lose sight of). The sovereignty of mothers, then. The sovereignty of mothers is most manifest—and most denied—in the capacity to harm and kill the child, born or unborn.[18] Mothers, who mother children but also mothers, and fathers too (the maternal contract is, as I have said, transgenerational), mothers can and do kill. We have long known—and taken for granted—that fathers kill. That they exercise their domestic and political sovereignty by killing their own children, and (more often) the children of others. But mothers kill too. They kill or intend to kill—they certainly fear to kill—children. They let them die. They have done so for centuries. Sarah and Jocasta were obviously ready to kill and in a way, not only in a psychoanalytic way, they did go through with it. Sovereignly so. Other mothers did it too. Mothers and slaves. And depending on the world in which such mothers, other mothers, live and die, the world in which they live still and die still, depending on the mothering of mothers, depending on the mothering of the village or of the world, mothers might also join in the killing of mothers, of other mothers, in the erasure or the enslavement, surely in the exploitation of mothers, and often themselves.[19] Still, the singular, if iterative, capacity to harm the child belongs to mothers, and it does as early as pregnancy, when "the mother is engaged in a furious battle with the fetus."[20] There is a capacity, a power, that is inherent to motherhood, and it is structurally related to, albeit different from, the maternal power to preserve.[21] It is a capacity that may take the form of fear or that of possession, property, and appropriation. Since Eve and Pandora, Sarah and Jocasta, not to mention Medea and Lady Macbeth; since the witch hunt, "killer nurses," "welfare queens" and other abortion activists, the sovereignty of mothers—the capacity to kill and destroy their offspring—has been known and even proclaimed ("Ja sam te rodila, ja ću te i ubiti!" in one, striking version). It has, more often been feared, denied, vilified, and deemed aberrant, horrifying, monstrous ("All psychoanalysts agree," wrote Simone de Beauvoir, "that mothers who are obsessed about harming their children, or who imagine horrible accidents, feel an enmity toward them they force themselves to repress").[22] It is a capacity that continues to be denied and fought, denied yet fought, but remains vastly unthought for its political—not exclusively or primarily criminal—significance, which, regardless of motivations, implicates the collective as a whole.[23] And it is surely a capacity that is dangerous to mothers themselves, highly and multifariously dangerous, in the United States and elsewhere, for those (unequal, always unequal) mothers, ultimately for all mothers, who *always put their own lives in danger* as they exercise or fail to exercise, *whether* they exercise or refrain from exercising, that capacity to kill, as they claim or deny the power to destroy.[24]

The power to kill and destroy. Here again, I seek neither to advocate nor condemn (recall the students' evaluation, which I opened with: good, bad), but I should mention that before deciding to write about mothers, I had embarked on a project—another cheerful project, my mother says—about destruction. Here and there, I have published segments of that project, but one thing that had motivated me was the realization that the language we use, the language academia uses, but also the language of law and economics, history and Marxism, is a language of making and of doing, of production and of construction, the social construction of everything. "Men make their own history," we (that is, not only men) happily repeat since Giambattista Vico and Karl Marx. The ubiquity of this prejudice to do and to make, to do it, just do it, is, like most of our modern prejudices about politics (about sovereignty or the social contract), waning. Or else it should be waning. It led me to wonder, in any case, about destruction and about the place we grant it, or fail to. What I found was quite surprising, but, most important for now, it has to do with the way theories of power, which culminated perhaps in Michel Foucault's formulations, distinguishing power as oppressive and coercive from power as productive and enabling, make little room for a modality of power that simply cannot be reduced or opposed to what power *does*. For there is a power that does not do, nor does it simply undo. There is *a power that destroys*. Better put, perhaps, destruction is its own form of power, its own kind of power. It has a distinct temporality (you can destroy a building in seconds, but never build one as fast). It is neither reversible nor correctable. It does not partake of, indeed, it exceeds a cycle where eggs turn into omelets and these turn into—what? eggs? (eggs are never to be retrieved nor restored). If there is a conservation of energy as modern physics keeps telling us, it does not mean that nothing is destroyed. Accordingly, and to pursue the asymmetry, destruction is distinct from violence (plastic today is among the single most destructive materials ever invented, yet it does its work without violence). Destruction is not only performed in times of war (where all the attention turns, ever so fleetingly), far from it. It rather accompanies—without resolving or reversing, much less redeeming—everything that Hannah Arendt called "labor, work, action." The specificity of destruction, of the power of destruction, has not made many philosophical or political head-lines, although its effects fill countless legal documents, history books and journalistic accounts. Increasingly so. Indeed, if history is the history of making and politics is about the making of worlds, then destruction has no place to speak of. It is exceptional. Or else it is "collateral damage." Destruction has, at any rate, taken little room in our thinking (as opposed to our collective effectivity), even if we know better than to ignore it. Elsewhere I have written about some preliminary steps toward a thinking of destruction found in the work of Martin Heidegger (after Nietzsche, certainly) and of Jacques Derrida, of Sigmund Freud and of Walter Benjamin too.[25] One of the most striking formulations I have found brought me back (or perhaps forward) to mothers, to the sovereignty of mothers and to the maternal contract. Here is Thomas Hobbes, who reiterated the matter in a number of places. First, *The Elements of Law.*

> The title to dominion over a child proceedeth not from the generation but from the preservation of it; and therefore in the estate of nature, the mother in whose power it is to save or destroy it, hath right thereto by that power. . . . And if the mother shall think fit to abandon, or expose her child to death, whatsoever man or woman shall find the child so exposed, shall have the same right which the mother had before; and for the same reason, namely for the power not of generating, but preserving.[26]

Hobbes pursues the same train of thought in *De Cive*, where he writes that "in the state of nature, every woman that bears children, becomes both a *mother* and a *lord*.... Wherefore original dominion over *children* belongs to the *mother*; and among men no less than other creatures, the birth follows the belly."[27]

Remarkably, Hobbes silently mobilizes the very possibility of constituting a collective that is neither multitude nor the commonwealth, yet suspends the war of all against all. Hobbes explains that, if the mother does raise the child ("because the state of nature is the state of war," Hobbes reminds us, as if we forgot), she must do it on one condition, "that being grown to full age he become not her enemy." Hobbes reiterates that man is an enemy to man, but he adds something crucial that has everything to do with sovereignty and with the social bond, with the possibility of constituting and preserving a collective. Hobbes describes a *maternal contract* (Carol Pateman comments, without elaborating, that "the infant must contract to obey her").[28] What Hobbes asserts is that "each man is an enemy to that other, whom he neither obeys nor commands," and so because "in the state of nature, every woman that bears children becomes both a *mother* and a *lord*," that is, someone who commands and must be obeyed.[29] Between mother and child, Hobbes therefore says, war—well beyond "the maternal-fetal conflict"—is already over.[30] Mothers, one might say, suspend the state of nature, the universal enmity that is the state of nature. And that suspension, that state of exception which is also the rule, is maternal sovereignty. One mother who is two, both mother and lord.

Finally, in *Leviathan*, Hobbes invokes, if negatively, the possibility of contractual relations, but places the maternal contract at their limit. Referring again to dominion over children, Hobbes writes that "if there be no Contract, the Dominion is in the

Mother ... seeing the Infant is first in the power of the Mother, so as she may either nourish, or expose it, if she nourishes it, it oweth its life to the Mother; and is therefore obliged to obey her, rather than any other; and by consequence the Dominion over it is hers."[31]

Many have written about these extraordinary lines, and I owe much to those who have discussed and disputed the relevance and even the significance of Hobbes's unusual position, which there is truly no reason to call feminist.[32] What should be obvious nonetheless is that Hobbes provides a striking confirmation of the maternal contract as that which binds mother and child, yes, but also two mothers, that is, two maternal functions, *two maternal powers*, that are clearly distinguished and, indeed, analytically and practically isolated from the power of generation, the power to give birth (Hobbes famously set that aside when he proposed, fictitiously enough, "to look at men as if they had just emerged from the earth like mushrooms and grown up without any obligation to each other").[33] In a manner that uniquely resonates in Benjamin's distinction between founding or instituting power— which Benjamin associates with preserving power (Hobbes's power of preservation)—and that other kind of power, a radically different, political power or *Gewalt*, which Benjamin identifies as divine, namely, destructive power. Incidentally, Benjamin elsewhere wrote of "the fullness" of his own mother's power, *die Machtvollkommenheit der Mutter*, as it was impressed upon him; Benjamin also described how, upon recovering from illness, "servants once more took the place of mother in my daily existence." Benjamin, as we already saw, upheld the figure of Niobe as a striking (if also vanishing) example of that distinct form of power he

called "mythical," thereby associated with the mother, as perpe-
trator and as victim. Mythical power (or legal violence), Benjamin says, "stopped short of claiming [the] mother's life."[34] It
certainly claimed her power, her sovereign power.

Hobbes, for his part, offered a theory of maternal power, of
maternal sovereignty, that, anticipating Benjamin, is clearly
double: preserving power and destructive power. Such is the
power of mothers, Hobbes says, their sovereign power (the
mother has dominion; she is lord and mother). As one commen-
tator puts it, "the relation of mother and child is the relation of
sovereign and subject. The mother is in fact the sovereign *avant
la lettre*."[35] More precisely, I think, "mothers are the first Hobbes-
ian sovereigns."[36]

And though Hobbes does not comment on that fact, he silently
establishes that sovereignty, *in the state of nature*, is divisible, substitutable, and indeed plural. For there are many mothers, and
every mother wields a double power. As he invokes Roman law
(the birth follows the belly), which would soon be formalized as
one of the foundations of American slavery (*partus sequitur ventrem*), Hobbes is inscribing in a singularly manifest way, the
dialectic of mother and slave, acknowledging the maternal contract, as a theory and a practice of sovereignty, of maternal
sovereignty.[37]

MOSES AS MOTHER

It would be an understatement to say that discussions of sovereignty have not taken mothers as their primary object.[38] Mothers,

as opposed to fathers, simply do not appear, or so for the most part, as we have just seen, in theorizations of sovereignty (or, in that essential pairing, in theories of enmity). Or of the political. A side note, a marginal note, at best. There has been no recognition either of a maternal contract, a contract that must be revocable, and the abrogation of which means the destruction of the child. Or of the mother.[39] Nor has anyone remarked on the strange reversal—one might even call it a rebuttal—of Hobbes's theorization by no less than Donald Winnicott, who located the power of destruction in the mother-child dyad, but granted it to the child rather than to the mother.[40] In this historical movement, this interminably extended moment, when mothers can be exposed and abandoned, starved and destroyed, when their lives and their freedom can be ceaselessly questioned and curtailed or worse, but when the lives of children (the unborn, that is) are deemed sacred—mothers and time—we may nevertheless find resources toward a different understanding, a different political understanding, in reflections on matricide, indeed, in a different grammar for what links matricide to infanticide and to abortion.[41] Social contract theorists, at any rate, have ignored the maternal contract, this crucial structure or infrastructure of collective existence over time. Finally, theorists of pastoral power, who have otherwise recognized Moses as a defining and exemplary figure, have failed to notice what one might call "the gender transitions in Moses' life," which are indeed striking.[42] This son of two mothers, as we have seen, understood and certainly expressed his own role and function—albeit in the mode of complaint—as maternal. Jesus as Mother? Try Moses and Monomaternalism.[43] The Hebrew, the Egyptian. The pastoral as maternal (though we must grant that the care it extends may conceal the true fate of the herd).

It begins with nourishment and with the flesh pots of Egypt. The Hebrews are longing for what they remember as the feeding fields of slavery, and they are weeping, one and all, weeping and whining, to their master and pastoral leader, they are weeping to God's servant, to Moses.

> Moses heard the people weeping, every clan apart, each person at the entrance of his tent. The Lord was very angry, and Moses was distressed. And Moses said to the Lord, "Why have You dealt ill with Your servant, and why have I not enjoyed Your favor, that You have laid the burden of all this people upon me? Did I conceive (*ha-anokhi hariti*, also: did I carry) all this people, did I bear them [*im anokhi yaldatihu*, also: did I give birth to it], that You should say to me, 'Carry them in your bosom as a nurse carries an infant [*ka-asher yissa ha-omen et ha-yonek*],' to the land that You have promised on oath to their fathers? Where am I to get meat to give to all this people, when they whine before me and say, 'Give us meat to eat!' I cannot carry all this people by myself, for it is too much for me. If You would deal thus with me, kill me rather, I beg You, and let me see no more of my wretchedness!"[44]

The mother and the slave are in constant proximity, entangled always. Moses, who has been fulfilling every maternal function he can (and those he cannot), has been but a slave and certainly a servant to the children of Israel. Or perhaps, very much like his mothers, he has been a nurse and indeed a mother.[45] Did he conceive them? Give birth to them? Carry them in his bosom like a nurse?[46] Carry them and feed them? Could he, could any mother, bear this burden alone?

Pastoral power, "the strangest form of power, the form of power that is most typical of the West," is, Michel Foucault says, as if talking (untypically enough!) about stereotypical mothers, "I think, entirely defined by its beneficence." Foucault is talking about Moses, about Moses the shepherd, Moses the mother (Foucault might have been reading Hobbes better, here, or else reconsidered his own biopolitical periodization).

> The shepherd is someone who feeds and who feeds directly, or at any rate, he is someone who feeds the flock first by leading it to good pastures, and then by making sure that the animals eat and are properly fed. Pastoral power is a power of care. It looks after the flock, it looks after the individuals of the flock, it sees to it that the sheep do not suffer, it goes in search of those that have strayed off course, and it treats those that are injured. A rabbinic commentary, which is a bit late but which absolutely reflects this, explains how and why Moses was chosen by God to lead the flock of Israel. It was because when Moses was a shepherd in Egypt he knew how to graze his sheep and knew, for example, that when he came to pasture he had to send the youngest sheep first to eat the most tender grass, then those a little older, and then the eldest and most robust who could eat the toughest grass. In this way each category of sheep had the grass it needed and enough to eat. Moses presided over this just, calculated, and reflected distribution of food.

Foucault goes on to say that

> pastoral power initially manifests itself in its zeal, devotion, and endless application. . . . The shepherd is someone who keeps watch. He "keeps watch" in the sense, of course, of keeping an eye out for possible evils, but above all in the sense of vigilance with regard to any possible misfortune. He will keep watch over the flock and avoid the misfortune that may threaten the least of its members. . . . The shepherd (*pasteur*) directs all his care towards others and never towards himself. . . . He does not even consider his own advantage in the well-being of his flock. I think we see here the appearance, the outline, of a power with an essentially selfless and, as it were, transitional character.

Finally, Foucault concludes, "the paradox of the shepherd is the problem of the sacrifice of the shepherd for his flock, the sacrifice of himself for the whole of his flock, and the sacrifice of the whole of his flock for each of the sheep."[47]

But Moses needs help mothering, and God will take it up. God, that other othermother, will provide, and mother the mother.[48] Or perhaps God mothers Moses because he is not quite the mother God is or would be? God—the mothers. There's a political theology! Contrary to Freud's claim, in any case, that Moses—greatest among sons, after all—was a (murdered) father, whom Freud wished to deprive the Jews of, Moses was at the very least an othermother.[49] Accordingly, God demonstrates what proper child care should look like, what mother care too, giving Moses *not one but seventy* helpers, seventy *comadres* that will share his burden

"Gather for Me seventy of Israel's elders of whom you have experience as elders and officers of the people, and bring them to the
Tent of Meeting and let them take their place there with you. I
will come down and speak with you there, and I will draw upon
the spirit that is on you and put it upon them; they shall share
the burden of the people with you, and you shall not bear it
alone."[50]

Moses, the pastoral mother, needs help. He needs help bearing and caring, carrying. He needs mothering in order to mother
the children. He cannot do it alone. That is a matter of life and
death. God, who here and elsewhere "appears as a feminine or
maternal figure," provides Moses with the care, the maternal
care he needs.[51] As Lisa Guenther puts it, "the maternity of Moses
and of God suggests one is not born, but rather *becomes* a mother."[52]
But I would go a little further. In fact, Guenther herself does as
she insists on the plurality of mothers. For "the figure of Moses
does not define the meaning of maternity so much as carry this
meaning over: from the God who commanded him, the biological mother who nursed him, the midwife who spared his life, the
stranger who adopted him, and the sister who assisted this."[53]
Beginning with the Hebrew, the Egyptian, the mother and the
slave, we are presented with a plurality of maternal functions, a
gathering of mothers, an arrangement whereby mothers substitute, complement, replace, and erase each other as parties to the
"same" maternal contract. The dialectic of mother and slave is a
kind of revolving door. Or a revolution. It includes, in any case, a
sovereign, a pastoral leader, a mother, and a slave, and more
mothers yet. The maternal contract is, as I have said, an unequal
one. It includes its own abrogation under the figures of maternal

death, the killing of offspring that is part and parcel of the maternal, of the destructive power of the mother. Sarah and Jocasta but also Hagar and Diotima certainly knew something about that power. Every mother in America, who has had or has considered having an abortion, and even those who have not, has had to confront the force of that power.[54] A power much more than a choice, more than an individual choice (as if the fate of the political as a whole was not thereby at stake!). And, against it, the violence of the powers that be, those Jacques Derrida rightly called "militants of death," and whose (terrifying) political vision goes well beyond the particular decision of individual mothers, the freedom or unfreedom of their individual bodies.[55] Every mother and othermother has had to consider the sovereignty of mothers, whether to affirm it, fear it, hide or deny it, and sometimes need and practice it. And not only in America.

MATRIA POTESTAS

As I have been arguing, the maternal contract provides an indispensable answer to the question: what is a village? Or: what is a nation, a people, a tribe, or a religion? It provides a way to understand anew, not "the origins and workings of society and government" but the very form of the collective—the state of its mothers and of its mothering—the conditions of its existence *over time*.[56] Now, it is an obvious, if cruel, component of any collective that maintains itself over time that it also grants itself the right to kill, the right to kill its own members and the right to kill others. "No society," that is, "can exist without some sexuality and some killing being outlawed; every prohibition entails allowance as its other side."[57] Collectives have delegated the right and the responsibility to kill, as well as the burden of guilt that is or may be associated with it, to individuals, groups, or professions, whose task it has been to perform the killing, which the collective deems necessary or simply right. Soldiers and doctors, priests, judges and executioners, police and immigration services have all been equipped with the authority and the instruments of death and destruction. These have been wielded legally and illegally over the course of human history, often with the claim that they are getting better, and more humane, with added justifications for the killing of innocents by way of necessity, (irreversible) judicial errors, or so-called collateral damage.[58] Some women, mothers, midwives, and nurses have occupied such positions, have had to perform those destructive—or eugenic, if there is a difference—functions, the very functions Hobbes attributed originally to mothers as sovereign. But few are the collectives who have taken responsibility for that excruciating responsibility; few have allowed, but rarely condoned, abortion and/or infanticide.[59] No collective I know of has delegated, officially delegated, to *mothers* the power to kill, the capacity, if not the authority, they always already exercise, that they must exercise, to take the measure of the world, to monitor the entry points, to guard the borders of the collective, to function as the immigration authorities and the border patrols, mediating the capacity of the collective to integrate, controlling the state of the maternal functions, the maternal capacities of the collective—or again, "the inhospitality of the world"[60]—when it comes to its youngest, and most vulnerable newcomers.[61] Yet, willingly or not, knowingly or not, mothers have had to exercise those very functions, forced and sometimes willing and able to wield that very power, under all too imaginable as well as unimaginable, unimaginably impossible, unsufferable circumstances. God knows mothers, killing mothers, have been vilified, made into some of our most famous monsters (Medea!) and worst criminals. Whoever denies that power, whoever seizes the power to kill—and there is no doubt that men, churches, and states have seized and usurped that power, monopolized the function of the border police, of judges and executioners, of those who let in or reject, often most violently, most destructively.[62] Doing so, they have deprived mothers yes, but they have also distorted and disdained the maternal contract upon which the collective depends. They have obfuscated the very maternal conditions of the collective's perdurance. Abortion is not about freedom of choice, and it is not a right. It speaks of a political vision. It enacts and practices the preservation, the duration of the collective as maternal. The sovereignty of mothers is about the power to kill, a power that, produced and reproduced over time, is intrinsic, intrinsically essential, to the maternal contract. There is nothing wild and savage about the sovereignty of mothers, and there is, it seems to me, every reason to take exception to what Anne Dufourmantelle, herself a fearless mother, claimed when she wrote that "savagery, in its ownmost madness, is maternal; it is what in a mother renders her capable of infanticide, but also capable of sacrificing her life for her child."[63] When committing that most common of crimes, as, for instance, Adrienne Rich and Toni Morrison reminded us, mothers have never turned mad or savage *alone*, or in the absence of world (they have done so, most often, in the absence of mothers and of mothering from the world). Neither have they done it, as far as I could find, as recognized agents of the collective to whom they belonged (even without belonging).[64] Yet the history of infanticide is long and crowded.[65] As long and crowded as the history of vilified mothers, punished for the state of the world into which they were supposed to give birth. Punished by the state. Unlike soldiers and executioners, judges and doctors, sovereigns and border patrols, mothers—those guardians who daily regulate the entry and the keeping of new members by the exercise of a great number of indispensable maternal functions (birthing, feeding, teaching, etc.)—have had to decide, or to fear, who was going to be let in (or not) and at what cost.[66] First of all, to themselves. Mother and slave, they have had to evaluate the state of the world, the kind of mothering the village or the mother country—the plantation—would provide for them. They have had to evaluate the state of the state, which, *pace* Virginie Despentes's otherwise compelling arguments, has hardly operated as "an all-powerful mother," but has rather abdicated a large array of maternal functions, leaving mothers, othermothers and yet others hanging in the most precarious of conditions.[67] And particularly so "in the wake," as Christina Sharpe writes, in the afterlife of slavery, and in the neoliberal dispensation under which we now live – or die. "Who will educate the educators?" asked Marx. Less implacably oriented toward the future, the maternal contract asks, "Who mothers the mothers?"[68] The village or the polity, the nation or the religion—these perform, have performed and must perform a number of maternal functions, which cannot be fulfilled by mothers alone, let alone by a lone and abandoned mother.

The collective then, is maternal. It is made and unmade by its mothers and mothering. It must be so made and unmade in order to perdure in time. Should it so perdure? The collective, any collective, is made and held, it has to be held, by a maternal contract, whereby maternal functions must be fulfilled, and mothers mothered. More or less well. More or less horribly. Mothers and slaves. But mothers must be mothered, as must children for as long as is needed to "train" them, as Sara Ruddick says ("caretaking always involves teaching the subjects of care").[69] And how long is that? Let us err, for now and once again, on the side of time. The reproduction—preservation and protection, growth and ritual reenactment—of any collective, of any grouping over time is dependent on the maternal contract, a contract that includes and wields, as it must, the destructive power of mothers, as every collective has, even if never acknowledging its maternal nature. Here too, here again, we are confronted with the duality of mothers, the plurality of maternal functions, which we might again summarize (after Derrida and Zakyyiah Iman Jackson) as "the beast and the sovereign" or as the mother and the slave.[70] "You got two feet, Sethe, not four," says Paul D.[71] What else did Toni Morrison's *Beloved* teach us?[72] I have done little else than learn Morrison's lesson, which terrifyingly illustrates that mothers respond to the world. And what a world this is. Mothers, which is to say, mothers and slaves, respond to—they mother—a world that mothers and more often fails to. Mothers write. They write according to a logic known as the logic of the *katechon*, which I earlier referred to as "maternal writing."[73] This is the sovereignty of mothers, who write and keep the world. Mothers guard and inscribe, they preserve and destroy. Mothers guard the world, they preserve it and also guard us from it. In time. Mothers keep the world and reproduce it (they write it). They keep the world, in time and for the time being. *In* that world, *for* that world and also safe *from* that world in which *we* live, in which they live and die, in which they mother and we all grow or die, grow and die, together and alone, mothers keep the world, they must keep the world at bay.[74] Mothers, *for now*, keep the end of the world at bay.

CODA

SOMETHING RATHER THAN NOTHING

BEFORE SHE BECAME the mother she already was, my mother was the youngest of five siblings, all born in Dar al-bayda, better known as Casablanca or Casa—the modern name of the ancient Berber port of Anfa. Hailing from a family of rabbis and merchants, her father was from Salé while her mother was from Gibraltar, which owes its name—Jebel Tariq—to Tariq Ibn Ziyad, who crossed the straits in 711. My mother was born in 1934, same as my father who, though from Tangiers, also grew up in Casablanca. In the French protectorate of Morocco, "Jews and Muslims lived adjacent to each other on certain streets and even in certain buildings. Violence between the communities was apparently not as frequent as in other cities. The Jewish population was extremely poor; although living within the city walls, some Jews lived in tents or the first bidonvilles."[1] Casablanca is where my parents met, both from large and partly shared Jewish social circles. This is where they went to school (at the Alliance

Israélite Universelle, that strange arm of the French *mission civil-isatrice*, which had opened its first school in 1862 Tetouan, and where my great-aunts taught, as did my mother, a brilliant student who went on to the *lycée* to complete her *baccalauréat).* Casablanca is where my parents were married, where they admittedly had their first sexual experience (not necessarily in that order, but who knows?). It is where they had their first-born, my elder brother, before exiling themselves, emigrating to France in 1961.[2] Within four quick but unspeakably difficult years, my parents had three more children, girl, boy, girl.

"Sabes muy bien que por ser la más chica de las mujeres a ti te corresponde cuidarme hasta el día de mi muerte" (You know per-fectly well that being the youngest daughter means you have to take care of me until the day I die).[3] My mother's mother—until recently, I had known her exclusively as Emilia or *Mémé*—did not utter this sentence, which I quote from Laura Esquivel's *Como agua para chocolate.* Not that I know. And yet, it certainly announces and summarizes a great deal of my mother's life, of her mothering styles too. A commanding figure, Emilia was an exile, a perfectly bilingual British subject—two mother tongues—from a Moroccan Jewish family (Jews had been allowed to set-tle in Gibraltar in the eighteenth century; most of them from Morocco, and likely Tetuan). In addition to Spanish and English, she seems to have learned French and Arabic when she settled in Casablanca, "to communicate with her sisters-in-law," my mother reluctantly reported, who implausibly insisted no Arabic was spo-ken in our family. My mother tells me all this in the perfect French of the *institutrice* she was, a language that was used interchangeably with Spanish as she was growing up. I could never figure out what my mother's mother tongue really was. I recently found out, in any case, that my grandmother's father, my great-grandfather Yehuda, must have spoken Portuguese, among other languages, as he was born in Cape Verde. Part of the larger Azores archipelago a few hundred miles off the West Coast of Africa, Cape Verde became, in the sixteenth century and up to the nineteenth, an important Portuguese commercial center, whose role in the slave trade is, sadly, well established. Like North African Muslims (or "Moors") who settled or transited there, the Jews of Cape Verde were apparently called *morenos*, even if some of them were rightly perceived as closer to the slaveholding and slave-trading *brancos*. So historians say, at least.[4] I mention this, in any case, because, along with this bit of information about my great-grandfather, I also found out that Emilia's first name was, in fact, Jamīla (spelled Yamila on her marriage contract), an Arabic name, evidently, which, like everything else Arabic or Berber, remained otherwise unspoken, that is, unspoken of, mostly, in my family.

I was raised very close to three of my grandparents (my Slāwi grandfather died in 1965 just a few months after emigrating), all of whom spoke Haquetía (a kind of Ladino that has more Arabic) or French or Spanish and (but, again, shush) Arabic and Moroccan Dārija. My grandparents had all died by the time I was twelve, even if they have stayed with me (I could explain to you how I still pray with my grandfather, still dance, a true possession, with my grandmother). Both my parents spoke, in French or in Spanish, calmly or excitedly, of Morocco as a very distant place to which nothing—less than nothing—connected us. And certainly not language, nor any mother tongue. Little was said, in any case, but the silence did not even seem to conceal much. Our primary, our only, belonging was that we were Jews. We were not French and we were not Moroccans. More important, we were Jews and *not* Arabs. The significance of this "not" and of a "*rien,* nothing" that binds and unbinds us and others, us to others, is one I am still trying to fathom. The negation of exile goes a long way.[5] I grew up, at any rate, in one of those *banlieues* that famously burned in 2005 (long after I had left; I had nothing to do with it). Immigrants were everywhere, North Africans in particular. I went to synagogue, just around the corner, and it was filled with, well, North African Jews, immigrants like us, all recently arrived. I went with increased frequency, delighted in the prayers, fascinated by the conversations in Arabic, the singing and talking in Hebrew and Arabic, the gestures and the melodies all preparing me for the Andalusi and Arabic music I would grow to love. My childhood friends share the same inheritance, the same music too. There was a strange clarity, therefore, to that message I kept receiving. Our upstairs neighbors might have been Moroccan Jews who spoke Arabic and Spanish, but we—we were not. We were just Jews. Not Moroccans, not Arabs. Although my father, just like Houria Bouteldja's father, liked to repeat that horrifying, colonial commonplace, "Les Arabes, c'est la dernière race après les crapauds" (Arabs are the last race after toads),[6] I associate the severity of that negation, the policing of that racialized border, with my mother, whom I knew to have been born and raised in Morocco, the country of my ancestors, depicted in the stories told (and in the food eaten, the screams yelled, the blessings uttered), in family gatherings, as Arab and Berber.

My mother, who asked me not to refer to her by name in this book ("Why do you need to write about me? What is there to tell?"), became, as I said, the mother of four. She mothered alone, mostly alone and almost alone, though never *completely* alone.[7] Beginning with her mother (Emilia/Jamīla), who soon became ill, however, and thus an added burden, my mother did have some of what we call "help." My father was there. He was (yes he was!), even if he was working very long hours every day. Still, although it happened and happens all the time, at any rate, no mother should have to do all the things my mother did, mostly alone, from the moment my siblings and I were born and earlier still. No one mother should have to do all these things, nor *could* she do all these things, without help, without some assistance or, finally, without a measure of acknowledgment. Without mothering and othermothering, in other words. Innumerable mothers have done just that, of course. They have done the impossible and beyond, engaged in countless forms of triumphant power and excruciating resourcefulness and more. Part of me wants to say that, to the extent that my mother more than fulfilled her end of what I have called the maternal contract, it is high time for me to hold my end of that exorbitant bargain. Or indeed, contract.

What I am trying to say is quite banal, I think, even if it should only make sense now, at the end of this book. I am trying to say that my mother is many. She contains multitudes, yes, but I want to underscore, in particular, that she always impressed me as being divided, as it were, two—at least. And like others, like Ella Shohat, I have long "tried to reconcile these two mothers," which my mother was and remains.[8] You may have gathered this from what I have already said by now, or you already knew it from your own experience ("maternal practice begins with a double vision," writes Sara Ruddick) or else from reading Melanie Klein, say.[9] "Everything has already happened, and the entire action takes place between the mother images."[10] Think good breast and bad breast, life and death—or think: the Jew, the Arab. My mother, incidentally, did not breastfeed me. She cared for me and fed me, but she also showed me, as I mentioned, a darker face. My mother frightened and threatened me. She was a hard person, she still is, and not only because she was, understandably, overwhelmed. She could not stand my tears, for instance, or accept my repeated refusals to eat. She sent me away and rejected me, leaving me alone and bereft many times ("at a certain moment the mother *withdraws*," writes Muraro, "just as God's Kabbala explains the creation of the world").[11] She loved me endlessly, still does, but there were limits, painful limits, interruptions, to her affection. She herself objects to this no doubt overdramatic description, but she did have a side I experienced as a form of hatred (I was projecting, you might say), and I blamed her for it for the longest time. How could she not have had limits? Under dire and often precarious conditions (we were, as I have said, exiles, recent immigrants; work and money were, to say the least, scarce), my mother raised four children in quick succession, while taking care of her mother and father, of her older sister, and of her husband too. She had tremendous patience, but she could also lose it, be driven mad (her words: *"folle, tu me rends folle!"*) by guilt and responsibility, by worry and fatigue. Not to mention: by us. That is, mostly, by me (you would never guess it now, but I am capable

of trying anybody's patience, even mothers'). And she was fight-
ing my father over education and over money. As he worked long
hours, my mother always seemed to me to rule and govern the
house. She appeared to me—and appears still—as a queen (from
her mother, my mother seems to have inherited a sense of "cultural superiority," something aristocratic and even arrogant,
something monarchical, at once Spanish and British, a sense of
chosenness you might wish to call Jewish. She is often told, out
of the blue, that she looks like the Queen of England).[12] For the
duration of my childhood and since, I found myself under "the
arbitrary, and not well defined, reign of the author of my life."[13]
I listened and obeyed and, most often, I confess, disobeyed, but
it was mostly her wishes and her commands that I heard and
internalized.

My mother was a queen, but she was also a servant. Like countless mothers, like Tita in Laura Esquivel's novel, she was constantly serving. She had started early, very early. She was, at any
rate, still and always feeding us, cleaning after us, teaching us,
catering to us, and doing everything for us, with us, constantly
effacing herself for us, subjecting herself to our wills and whims,
though hardly giving up on discipline. She diminished herself
often, very often, in words and in deeds. She—one of the sharp-
est and quickest, most intelligent persons I know—called herself
"stupid" (*bête, idiote*) on a daily basis. To this day, moreover, she
refers to herself as a kind of nothing (*rien*), again, as having done
nothing (*je n'ai rien fait*), given or transmitted nothing (*je ne vous
ai rien donné*). Should you listen to her, you would think that she
fed us nothing either, taught us nothing, left us nothing. "—
Rien.—Rien?—Rien. C'était toujours la même chose, avec moi.

Rien."[14] This *rien*, this nothing is one I associated early on with the nothing of our Moroccan past I mentioned earlier, with the *not* of our not-being-Arab. I think of it now as the knot of our souls, as Stefania Pandolfo calls it.[15] Be that as it may, my mother is everything to me, while for herself, she is nothing (she still insists that my audience will be bored to death in hearing or reading what I am saying about her). I'll repeat that my mother is a queen. And also that she is a servant. Less than a servant, for herself, for not recognizing it herself. Mother and slave. Once again, my mother was born and raised in Morocco, but, like my father, she acknowledges neither debt nor influence, no true connection with the complex life and history I have sketched. In a way that Émile Ajar enabled me to begin parsing, I knew that we were not French, as I was growing up, which was true enough, but neither had we been Moroccans, Berbers, or Chleuh, certainly not Arabs nor *morenos* (my *Tanjawi* father, in true Athenian fashion, affectionately called my mother by the local equivalent of a Barbarian, *forastera*). We were Jews, and—most emphatically in a freshly postcolonial France—we were *not* Arabs, something I have long felt and understood for myself as an intense proximity, the proximity of exile, to Arabs. Like Albert Swissa (like Émile Ajar, too), I thus live and love with my "longings to Ishmael"[16]—and to Hagar, "the essence of all images of exile." "Zion is Hagar," writes Amnon Raz-Krakotzkin, screaming in the wasteland that grows, "and Hagar is Zion."[17] And so I live, I let myself go on living, with the duality of mothers. A queen and a servant, a queen and an exile. A Jew and (not) an Arab. Sarah or Hagar. Or both. And so you might say, paraphrasing C. L. R. James, that these are my mothers; these are my people. They are yours too, if you want them.[18]

HAGAR AND SARAH

In the state of nature—the growing and asymmetric wars—that all too clearly defines both domestic and national (the waning of which is increasingly visible too) and certainly international relations, there are many mothers, many a motherland and also, *pro patria mori*, many a fatherland.[19] There are queer lands too, like France's *mère patrie* or Greece.[20] There is Mother India, Mother Russia, there is Egypt, the land of Egypt, and *knesset israel,* the Jewish *moledet*, the Islamic *ummah.* These are indeed problems, Howard Eilberg-Schwartz explained, problems "for men in monotheism."[21] For men and nationalism too. One such problem is monomaternalism, which obfuscates and hides the maternal contract. For better or for worse (these days, it is mostly for worse), I want to conclude with this image of lands, countries, and collectives, those we call nations still, but also races and religions, and, as if these were more consistently familiar and familial, tribes. I want to conclude with the notion that there are many mothers, many maternal contracts that have preserved such collectives. For how long? Part of the way in which we think of violence and oppression, of conflict and war, is no doubt governed by a logic of fathers, brothers, and, in any case, enemies. Maternal thinking, maternal being, is not—I can't agree with Sara Ruddick—peace. But to think the maternal, to live the political as maternal, entails the knowledge, the very political knowledge, that there is never only one mother. It is therefore not, as Albert Camus thought, that I have to choose between justice or my mother, justice after my mother.[22] It is rather that there is no justice for us, no justice for any collective, *no justice without mothers.* Nor are there mothers without (some) justice: for we, we the people, are nothing without mothers and mothering. We the people (the nation or the race, the tribe or the religion) are mothers. We must finally become the mothers we have always been. If we are to perdure, that is. We, we who call ourselves a "we" *in time,* do fulfill and must fulfill an indispensable number of maternal functions. More important, and not unlike Moses and every other mother, every othermother, *we cannot do this alone.* No one ever has. No mother has ever mothered in the absence of village or world, without othermothers. Moses himself, remember, needed seventy elders!

Appropriately enough, the Jewish tradition holds that there are seventy nations. This means that no nation is an island. No nation, no collective is a *single* mother. There are many mothers, within and without the nation that is, itself, a mother (or two). What we might have to learn, therefore, and confront too, is that this condition, the maternal contract, between and within nations, between entities that must be conceived as maternal— this condition is unequal. It certainly has been and continues to be. The mother and the slave. Hagar and Sarah. Or, as I have put it elsewhere, the Jew, the Arab (Plato had proposed the Greek, the Persian—two mothers for any functioning polity). How to understand—not to mention resolve—the obvious inequality at play is, obviously, a difficult task, if not an impossible one—or many. Not unlike mothering.

King Solomon's judgment must be reconsidered, therefore, from the perspective of the mothers, the two mothers. For the issue is not simply the future of the living child or the recognition of the true mother. The issue is rather double, it is "either the love split in two by the sword or the living child."[23] The judgment or the resolution, justice itself, as it were, is less whether the child can be cut in two than the maternal love, the maternal contract, that is here at stake, at play and on display. And one question the judgment must contend with is whether *the two mothers can be separated*. Could they ever part from each other, from their dual and divided, their shared maternality? "We inhabit the same house (*yoshvot be-bayit eḥad*)," says the first mother, "and I gave birth with her (*va-eledᶜima*)." The other woman, the other mother "also gave birth," so the first mother narrates, while insisting on their shared living arrangements, on their shared house (the word *bayit*, house, is repeated four times within the two verses I quote), their shared maternality. "We are together (*ve-anaḥnu yaḥdav*); there is no one else in the house except for us; we are two in the house."[24] The two mothers (figures for one contested piece of land, in Bertolt Brecht's version) are both mothers, and they form one home, one polity.[25] Mother of the living and mother of the dead, neither is a *truer* mother (they are said to be prostitutes, like Madame Rosa, that prodigious othermother in Émile Ajar's *La vie devant soi*). In life and in death, in life and after death (for one mother did kill her child by laying on it), the two mothers will return to the house they inhabit together. Even if separated by a verdict (or by a security fence), they are bound, bound by maternal sovereignty and by a maternal contract, which transcend the wisdom of the king, and the future of the Child, but implicate the very unnatural nature of the collective they form. Indeed, a shadow version of the trial of the mothers, a second iteration of the story of the two mothers shows them bound by yet another terrifying contract—a totemic meal, a shared substance—the shared eating of their babies.[26] This time, the time of war and of famine, the time of "self-devouring growth," the king shows himself unable to render judgment,[27] There is no child to save, no human society left of which this would be "the earliest state," and the world of the two mothers is a devastated world.[28] Yet it must be lived, and justice must be rendered. For which mothers? For which of the two stories of mothers? A story—a mother—of and for the living, a story—a mother—of and for the dead.

We have all been mothered. More or less well. More or less *by our own mothers*. By two mothers, then, by two mothers at least ("She was like a second mother to me . . . Third to be precise"),[29] who make and preserve, who reproduce the political economy of motherhood, as they do the unequal sovereignty of peoples and nations, and the unequal powers of destruction to which I have attended. Collectives, in order to exist in time, require mothers. They require mothering. *They are mothers who mother mothers.* More or less well. In life and in death (as Momo, the Arab Muslim child of *La vie devant soi*, knows too, raised as he is, not by his mother, long dead, but by a living—and dying—Holocaust survivor, Madame Rosa). In life and through death, which is to say, in time. For that fact, that undeniable political fact, is not a beginning, nor is it a foundation. It is a continuation, the very condition of possibility and impossibility of preservation and of destruction. It is a repetition and an iteration. There are mothers, therefore, two mothers at least, so that mothers mother mothers. For now. And who knows for how long? Locally or globally, then, and today still, if provisionally, there are mother and slave, Hagar and Sarah. The Jew, the Arab.

Hebrew and Arabic, by the way, seem to share a word that designate the collective or collectives that we still are. The proximity of the two words, and the meaning that resonates—it is a matter of sound and of sounding—is almost speculative, even if it goes back a long way across texts and centuries. That word, which I mentioned earlier in passing, is *ummah/ummah*. It means and does not mean "mother," and very much sounds like it. We are mothers, the so-called Semitic languages would be saying or sounding to us. Not mother tongues, not yet, not only, and not fatherlands either. We, insofar as we are a we, we Jews and Arabs, we are mothers.[30] Mother and slave. Mothers of the living and mothers of the dead. Ah! the dead. Just as James Baldwin taught, whom I might quote again, with a maternal twist in his maternal spirit. "If we—and now I mean [those] who must, like mothers, insist on, or create, the consciousness of the others—do not falter in our duty now, we may be able, handful that we are, to end the . . . nightmare, and achieve our country, and change the history of the world."[31]

Mother-work is work, I wrote earlier. It is dream-work and nightmare-work, mourning work.

Where else, then? Where else would we find a song to that maternal presence, to the *Shekhina*, the divine presence who, *exiled in the Holy Land,* is at once a mother and a slave, Hagar and Sarah both, queen and servant, *knesset israel,* the peoples of the land, the mothers of the land? Where else would we find Palestine? That "piece of the Palestinian fate that would confuse even King Solomon?"[32] Where else would we find justice *and* mothers, and an appeal to the becoming of mothers, the duality of mothers, repetitions, iterations of mothers and of mothering ("But I have to tell you that I've never known where it all began and where it ends, because in my opinion it just keeps going on"), than in a poem by, in the maternal writing of, the Palestinian poet, one who has gone the farthest to think and speak together the Jew, the Arab?[33] I shall conclude with Mahmoud Darwish, with his words, in translation.

> Give birth to me again. . . . Give birth to me again that I may know
> in which land I will die, in which land I will come to life again.
> Peace be unto you as you light the morning fire, peace be unto you, peace be unto you.
> Isn't it time for me to give you some presents, to return to you?
> Is your hair still longer than our years, longer than the trees of clouds
> stretching the sky to you so they can live?
> Give birth to me again so I can drink the homeland's milk from you and
> remain a child in your arms, remain a child.

CODA

For ever. I have seen many things, mother, I have seen. Give
   birth to

me again, so that I may remain in your hands.

When you feel love for me, do you still sing and cry about
   nothing?

Mother, I have lost my hands

On the waist of a woman of a mirage. I embrace sand, I
   embrace a shadow. Can I come back to you/to myself?

Your mother has a mother, the fig tree in the garden has
   clouds.

Don't leave me alone, a fugitive. I want your hands

To carry my heart. I long for the bread of your voice,
   mother!

I long for everything. I long for myself . . . I long for you.[34]

NOTES

PREFACE

1. "Man is born free," Jean-Jacques Rousseau wrote, whom I adapt here, "and everywhere he is in chains." Jean-Jacques Rousseau, "The Social Contract," book 1, chapter 1, trans. Donald A. Cress, in Rousseau, *Basic Political Writings* (Indianapolis: Hackett, 1987), 141.

2. Thomas Hobbes, *On the Citizen,* Richard Tuck, ed. (Cambridge: Cambridge University Press, 1998), 102.

3. "But I have to tell you that I've never known where it all began and where it ends, because in my opinion it just keeps going on." Emile Ajar, *Momo (Life Before Us)*, trans. Ralph Manheim (Garden City: Doubleday, 1978), 143; translation altered.

4. Luisa Muraro, *The Symbolic Order of the Mother,* trans. Francesca Novello (Albany: State University of New York Press, 2018), 18.

5. Isaiah 49:23.

6. Marina Warner, *Alone of All Her Sex: The Myth and the Cult of the Virgin Mary* (Oxford: Oxford University Press, 2013).

7. Andrea Freeman, "Unmothering Black Women: Formula Feeding as an Incident of Slavery," *Hastings Law Journal* 69 (August 2018): 1545–1606.

8. Sarah Knott, *Mother Is a Verb: An Unconventional History* (New York: Picador, 2019).

9. Iris Murdoch, *The Sovereignty of Good* (London: Routledge, 2014), 82; and compare what Timothy Campbell and Grant Farred call "selving" or what happens when, apparently void of mother, "the I is dispossessed of its mine or mines," when "the unequal emerges," which is, for them, "the incompatibility and the incommensurability of the self with the act of possessing itself." Timothy Campbell and Grant Farred, *The Comic Self: Toward Dispossession* (Minneapolis: University of Minnesota Press, 2023), 77.

10. Murdoch, *The Sovereignty of Good,* 14.

11. I am less interested in the good (or the bad) than Murdoch was, but I do note she wrote that "goodness appears to be both rare and hard to picture. It is perhaps most convincingly met with in simple people—inarticulate, unselfish mothers of large families—but these cases are also the least illuminating" (51–52).

12. "Who is even interested today," Romain Gary asked in a radio interview, "in the mother, in mothers, in the relationship of a son to his mother? No one cares!" Romain Gary, "L'enfant de sa mère," podcast, www.radiofrance.fr/franceculture/podcasts/a-voix-nue/l-enfant-de-sa-mere-4178323; and see Roland Barthes, *Camera Lucida: Reflections on Photography,* trans. Richard Howard (New York: Hill and Wang, 1981), 69–70; and Barthes, *Mourning Diary,* trans. Richard Howard (New York: Hill and Wang, 2010). As a young teenager, I devoured Ajar's *La vie devant soi,* a novel written by Romain Gary but published under the pseudonym Émile Ajar.

13. Jacques Derrida, "Circumfession," in Geoffrey Bennington and Jacques Derrida, *Jacques Derrida,* trans. Geoffrey Bennington (Chicago: University of Chicago Press, 1993).

14. The Gospel of Luke 14; The Gospel of Matthew 12.

15. A song by the band Pink Floyd from their album *The Wall.*

16. Not Darren Aronofsky's, rather Roger Mitchell's.

17. As Iris Marion Young writes, "mother and daughter are also strange to one another, surprised at how it seems they are for the other." Iris Marion Young, *Intersecting Voices: Dilemmas of Gender, Political Philosophy, and Policy* (Princeton: Princeton University Press, 1997), 47; and see, *inter alia,* Andrea O'Reilly, ed., *Mothers and Sons: Feminism, Masculinity, and the Struggle to Raise Our Sons* (New York: Routledge, 2001); Marianne Hirsch, *The Mother/Daughter Plot: Narrative, Psychoanalysis, Feminism* (Bloomington: Indiana University Press, 1989), and many more since.

18. Kyoo Lee, *Reading Descartes Otherwise: Blind, Mad, Dreamy and Bad* (New York: Fordham University Press, 2013), 19; for Jean-Joseph Goux, Descartes

surely repeats Oedipus's journey. His is "no longer the thought of a son who still defines himself relationally as son of a father, it is the thought of a son who has deliberately and consciously orphaned himself, disinherited himself, who has made himself the son of no one." Jean-Joseph Goux, *Oedipus, Philosopher*, trans. Catherine Porter (Stanford: Stanford University Press, 1993), 160.

19. Susan R. Bordo repeatedly identifies Descartes' world as "mother-world" in *The Flight to Objectivity: Essays on Cartesianism and Culture* (Albany: State University of New York Press, 1987).

20. https://pen.org/a-kentucky-of-mothers/.

21. "Time is a mother" is Ocean Vuong's beautiful phrase, another mourning diary. Ocean Vuong, *Time Is a Mother* (New York: Penguin, 2022).

22. Elissa Marder demonstrates the lasting and "uncanny technological conception of the maternal function" in *The Mother in the Age of Mechanical Reproduction: Psychoanalysis, Photography, Deconstruction* (New York: Fordham University Press, 2012), 8.

23. Orna Donath, *Regretting Motherhood: A Study* (Berkeley: North Atlantic, 2017) includes an important discussion of motherhood and time.

24. Joan Cocks, *On Sovereignty and Other Political Delusions* (London: Bloomsbury, 2014), 12.

25. Iris Marion Young, *On Female Body Experience: "Throwing Like a Girl" and Other Essays* (Oxford: Oxford University Press, 2005), 89.

26. See Carol Pateman and Charles W. Mills, *Contract and Domination* (Cambridge: Polity, 2007), who both revisit their respective arguments on the social contract and the racial contract but, not untypically, give little thought to mothers.

27. Since Johann Jakob Bachofen's 1861 *Das Mutterrecht* and by way of Robert Briffault's 1927 *The Mothers*, the notion of an originary, women-ruled society has had ambivalent success, and remains unpersuasive. Cynthia Eller, *Gentlemen and Amazons: The Myth of Matriarchal Prehistory, 1861–1900* (Berkeley: University of California Press, 2011); and see Eller's previous work, *The Myth of Matriarchal Prehistory: Why an Invented Past Won't Give Women a Future* (Boston: Beacon, 2000), addressing the feminist reception.

28. Carla Freccero is the only scholar I found who uses this phrase, which I will try to set to work. Freccero articulates a—still unheeded—call to introduce "maternal sovereignty into our accounts of nation-state formation." Carla Freccero, "Voices of Subjection: Maternal Sovereignty and

Filial Resistance in and Around Marguerite de Navarre's *Heptameron*," *Yale Journal of Law and the Humanities* 5, no. 1 (1993): 147–57.

29. Jessamine Chan, *The School for Good Mothers: A Novel* (New York: Simon and Schuster, 2022); Lee Edelman, *No Future: Queer Theory and the Death Drive* (Durham: Duke University Press, 2004).

30. Mary G. Dietz, "Citizenship with a Feminist Face: The Problem with Maternal Thinking," *Political Theory* 13, no. 1 (February 1985): 21; and see Patricia Boling, "The Democratic Potential of Mothering," *Political Theory* 19, no. 4 (November 1991): 606–25

31. Janice Doane and Devon Hodges, *From Klein to Kristeva: Psychoanalytic Feminism and the Search for the "Good Enough" Mother* (Ann Arbor: University of Michigan Press, 1992).

32. Nancy Chodorow famously asks about "the way women's mothering is reproduced across generations" and "how women today come to mother." Nancy Chodorow, *The Reproduction of Mothering: Psychoanalysis and the Sociology of Gender* (Berkeley: University of California Press, 1978), 3–4. I rather attend to the way mothering reproduces and preserves the collective across generations. The most self-evident—and misleading—assertion that "we want to start a family" must contend with earlier beginnings and with the absence of an expiration date. Families or nations, in other words, which is to say, collectives in general, all-too thoughtlessly "glide into a limitless future." Benedict Anderson, *Imagined Communities: Reflections on the Origin and Spread of Nationalism* (New York: Verso, 2006), 12.

33. Although she is preoccupied with the *undoing* of the collective, and does not speak of mothers or of motherhood, Ninon Grangé offers an important and proximate formulation "Identity in the political sense," she writes, "signifies permanency and reproduction. The duration of the political entity determines its existence . . ." Ninon Grangé, *De la guerre civile* (Paris: Armand Colin, 2009), n.p..

34. Always an inspiration, Donna Haraway proposes that "every technology is a reproductive technology." Donna Haraway, "The Promises of Monsters: A Regenerative Politics for Inappropriate/d Others" in, Lawrence Grossberg, Cary Nelson, and Paula A. Treichler, eds., *Cultural Studies* (New York: Routledge, 1992], 299. Emanuele Coccia urges us to "begin to see what we call 'technics' above all as a variation on what takes place in motherhood. It is because living beings are capable of giving birth—because they can become mothers—that we can manipulate the world, transform it, make

the world participate in this metamorphic momentum that we call life." Emanuele Coccia, *Metamorphoses,* trans. Robin Mackay (Cambridge: Polity, 2021), 29.

35. The dominant association of mothering with birth remains pervasive. Whether the technological transformations we are witnessing (perhaps less novel than they seem, as we shall see) usher in a "motherless age" is, of course an important question; see, e.g., Dana S. Belu, *Heidegger, Reproductive Technology, and the Motherless Age* (Cham, Switzerland: Palgrave Macmillan, 2017), or, with a different but no less depressing view, Michelle Goodwin, *Policing the Womb: Invisible Women and the Criminalization of Motherhood* (Cambridge: Cambridge University Press, 2020).

36. Unlike Rousseau and many others before and after him, I do not seek to prescribe (or so very little, I swear). Very much like him (and perhaps with a secret nod to Hannah Arendt as well), I shall ask about the entanglement of sovereignty and slavery. "Can liberty be maintained only with the support of servitude?" Rousseau asked. And answered: "Perhaps." Rousseau, "The Social Contract," book 3, chapter 15, 199.

37. The slogan Maggie Nelson quotes, discussing Lee Edelman. Maggie Nelson, *The Argonauts* (Minneapolis: Graywolf, 2015), 75.

38. See, e.g., Mary Jacobus, *First Things: The Maternal Imaginary in Literature, Art, and Psychoanalysis* (New York: Routledge, 1995).

39. "Feminist Politics Still Needs Motherhood," writes Amanda Watson in her contribution to a rich collection of essays that still juxtaposes motherhood *and* politics: Amanda Watson, in Lucy B. Hall, Anna L. Weissman, and Laura J. Shepherd, eds., *Troubling Motherhood: Maternality in Global Politics* (Oxford: Oxford University Press, 2020), 179; and see Cesare Casarino and Andrea Righi, eds., *Another Mother: Diotima and the Symbolic Order of Italian Feminism* (Minneapolis: University of Minnesota Press, 2018).

40. Pascale Molinier, Sandra Laugier, and Patricia Paperman, "Introduction," in *Qu'est-ce-que le care? Souci des autres, sensibilité, responsabilité* (Paris: Payot & Rivages, 2021).

41. Sara Ruddick puts it limpidly when she writes that "whatever difference might exist between female and male mothers, there is no reason to believe that one sex rather than the other is more capable of doing maternal work." Sara Ruddick, *Maternal Thinking: Toward a Politics of Peace* (Boston: Beacon, 1995), 41; Ruddick goes on to underscore that "throughout the world women not only have borne but have disproportionally cared for children" (41).

42. I shall return to the groundbreaking contribution made by Hortense J. Spillers in her "Mama's Baby, Papa's Maybe: An American Grammar Book" in Spillers, *Black, White, and in Color: Essays on American Literature and Culture* (Chicago: University of Chicago Press, 2003); and see Sara Clarke Kaplan, *The Black Reproductive: Unfree Labor and Insurgent Motherhood* (Minneapolis: University of Minnesota Press, 2021).

INTRODUCTION

1. Sigmund Freud, *Civilisation and Its Discontent*, trans. Joan Riviere, in *The Standard Edition of the Complete Psychological Works,* James Strachey, ed. (London: Hogarth and Institute of Psycho-Analysis, 1961), 21:91.

2. "In the 'child-text' it is a *mother* who writes of her experiences: childbirth, playing with her infant, watching over the child sick for the first time, feeling separated from and at the same time united with the child, memories of her own mother . . . her relationship to language, to the Law." Susan Rubin Suleiman, "Writing and Motherhood," in Shirley Nelson Garner Claire Kahane and Madelon Sprengnether, eds, *The (M)other Tongue: Essays in Feminist Psychoanalytic Interpretation.* (Ithaca: Cornell University Press, 1985), 369.

3. There are too many references to mention, although I will refer to a few. For now, I'll single out Emma Lieber, who summarizes it best in one chapter title, "On Coming to Write, Or Tell Me About Your Mother." Emma Lieber, *The Writing Cure* (New York: Bloomsbury, 2020), 1–41.

4. Maggie Nelson quotes an article that begins with "No subject offers a greater opportunity for terrible writing than motherhood." Maggie Nelson, *The Argonauts* (Minneapolis: Graywolf, 2015), 71. Fear and trembling. But Nelson quotes on: "To be fair, writing well about children is tough." Still, I must interject, who said that writing about motherhood was the same as writing about children??

5. Tiphaine Samoyault, *"Birth Pangs:* La traduction comme procréation," in *Po&sie* 137–38 (2011): 44–50; Walter Benjamin suggests that there is something maternal about translation, for translation is what changes the mother tongue of the translator, having "the special mission of watching over the maturing process of the original language and the birth pangs of its own." Walter Benjamin, "The Task of the Translator," trans. Harry Zohn, in Benjamin, *Selected Writings 1,* Marcus Bullock and Michael

Jennings, eds. (Cambridge, Mass.: Belknap Press of Harvard University Press, 1996), 256.

6. Eva Feder Kittay, *Love's Labor: Essays on Women, Equality and Dependency* (New York: Routledge, 2020); to my embarrassment, I had not read Kittay at the time I gave my lectures, but I want to hope that my arguments will be read as following in her path.

7. Michelle Boulous Walker, *Philosophy and the Maternal Body: Reading Silence* (New York: Routledge, 1998), 92–95; On "maternal impressions," often starting with dreams, see *inter alia* Marie-Hélène Huet, *Monstrous Imagination* (Cambridge, Mass.: Harvard University Press, 1993) and Margrit Shildrick, "Maternal Imagination; Reconciling First Impressions," *Rethinking History: The Journal of Theory and Practice* 4, no. 3 (2000): 243–60; a different take can be found in Sarah S. Richardson, *The Maternal Imprint: The Contested Science of Maternal-Fetal Effects* (Chicago: University of Chicago Press, 2021).

8. I refer to Freud's famous account of the "dream-work" in *The Interpretation of Dreams*, which involves wish fulfillment as well as displacement, distortion, and condensation; one particular Freudian dream has been much written about, namely, "Father, Can't You See I'm Burning?" or "Dream of the Burning Child."

9. See Yali Hashash, *Whose Daughter Are You? Ways of Speaking Mizrahi Feminism* [in Hebrew] (Bnei Brak: Hakibbutz Hameuchad, 2022), 307.

10. Fred Moten, *In the Break: Aesthetics of the Black Radical Tradition* (Minneapolis: University of Minnesota Press, 2003), 17.

11. Is my mother mine? Am I my mother's? "How can you care for something that is not yours?" ask Campbell and Farred: Timothy Campbell and Grant Farred, *The Comic Self: Toward Dispossession* (Minneapolis: University of Minnesota Press, 2023), 9. I register the significance of "dispossession," what Campbell and Farred call "the comic self" in a book written against property and possession, but also against "the fallacy of self-possession in the toddler" (6), and in the total absence of mothers, unless one attempts to decipher "these moments of toddler parenting" (8).

12. Shuli Barzilai, *Lacan and the Matter of Origins* (Stanford: Stanford University Press, 1999), 136.

13. "But is not a mark, wherever it is produced, the possibility of writing?" asks Derrida. See Jacques Derrida, *Of Grammatology*, trans. Gayatri Chakravorty Spivak (Baltimore: Johns Hopkins University Press, 1997), 302;

Derrida's arguments about writing do not have to be made more explicit here, though they are essential. And essential too the significance of maternality and motherhood in Derrida's own writing and formulations, as I tried to explain in Gil Anidjar, "Solicitude" in *Derrida Today* 16, no. 1 (2023): 3–19.

14. Dorothy Roberts, *Killing the Black Body: Race, Reproduction, and the Meaning of Liberty* (New York: Pantheon, 1997), 20; and see Marga Vicedo, *The Nature and Nurture of Love: From Imprinting to Attachment in Cold War America* (Chicago: University of Chicago Press, 2013); on tradition, see Talal Asad, "The Idea of an Anthropology of Islam," *Occasional Papers, Center for Contemporary Arab Studies*, Georgetown University, 1986.

15. *La mère en moi*, "the mother in me," is, I was surprised to discover, the title of the French translation of Sheila Heti's book, *Motherhood* (New York: Henry Holt, 2018). It is a striking title for a book that (before Britney Spears's recent and most famous contribution) narrates the path of a writer who, undoubtedly inhabited or indeed haunted by mothers (her own mother no less than her own self as a mother), wonders, "can a woman who makes books be let off the hook by the universe for not making the living thing we call babies?" In a different register, Donald Winnicott describes the stomach as "rather like a miniature good mother inside." Donald Winnicott, *The Child, the Family and the Outside World* (Cambridge, Mass: Perseus, 1987), 36. More important, finally, is the conception of a collective, of a community who would have been "handed the specific occasion to learn *who* the female is within itself," which is to say here, "the heritage of the mother," to be regained as an aspect of (collective) personhood. Hortense J. Spillers, "Mama's Baby, Papa's Maybe: An American Grammar Book," in Spillers, *Black, White, and in Color: Essays on American Literature and Culture* (Chicago: University of Chicago Press, 2003), 228.

16. Iris Marion Young, *On Female Body Experience: "Throwing Like a Girl" and Other Essays* (Oxford: Oxford University Press, 2005), 46; unlike Young, I shall not restrict my argument to the pregnant mother, to what she calls "pregnant embodiment."

17. "As long as mothers have been responsible for their children, they have been blamed for inadequately fulfilling their responsibilities," write Beverly Birns and Niza Ben-Ner, in "Psychoanalysis Constructs Motherhood," in Beverly Birns and Dale F. Hay, eds., *The Different Faces of Motherhood* (New York: Springer Science+Business Media, 1988), 58.

18. Quoted in Barzilai, *Lacan and the Matter of Origins*, 45.
19. Nelson, *The Argonauts*, 20.
20. Selma Fraiberg, *Every Child's Birthright: In Defense of Mothering* (Toronto: Bantam, 1977).
21. Edward W. Said, *Orientalism* (New York: Vintage, 1978); Said quotes Karl Marx's *Eighteenth Brumaire*.
22. Gilles Deleuze, "Coldness and Cruelty," trans. Jean McNeil, in *Masochism* (New York: Zone, 1991), 20.
23. Deleuze, 63; Hendrika Freud confirms that "certain men remain bound to their (inner) mother and strongly identify with her." Hendrika C. Freud, *Men and Mothers: The Lifelong Struggle of Sons and Their Mothers,* trans. Marjolijn de Jager (London: Karnac, 2013), xxiv; and see Jay Watson, "Guys and Dolls: Exploratory Repetition and Maternal Subjectivity in the Fort/Da Game," *American Imago* 52, no. 4 (Winter 1995): 463–503.
24. I first heard of maternal microchimerism, also known as maternal fetal microchimerism in Alice Diop's extraordinary film *Saint Omer* (Les Films du Losange, 2022), to which my own book may turn out to be no more than an extended footnote; for a brief account, see www.nytimes.com/2015/09/15/science/a-pregnancy-souvenir-cells-that-are-not-your-own.html, accessed February 21, 2023.
25. Talal Asad, "Thinking About Religion Through Wittgenstein," *Critical Times* 3, no. 3 (December 2020): 407; and see Stefania Pandolfo, *Knot of the Soul: Madness, Psychoanalysis, Islam* (Chicago: University of Chicago Press, 2018).
26. Anne O'Byrne, *Natality and Finitude* (Bloomington: Indiana University Press, 2010); Hans-Georg Gadamer, *Truth and Method,* trans. Joel Weinsheimer and Donald G. Marshall (London: Continuum, 2004).
27. Elisabeth Schüssler-Fiorenza, *In Memory of Her: A Feminist-Theological Reconstruction of Christian Origins* (New York: Crossroads, 1994); "Repetition and recollection are linked as an ambiguity," write Campbell and Farred about "the comic self out of which emerges the possibility of a different outcome and perhaps a different world" (Campbell and Farred, *The Comic Self*, 39). I shall side with maternality rather than natality.
28. "The father of the *logos* is also a mother," writes Jill Frank, commenting on Plato. Jill Frank, *Poetic Justice: Rereading Plato's Republic* (Chicago: University of Chicago Press, 2018), 25; and see Anidjar, "Solicitude."
29. Elizabeth Grosz, *Volatile Bodies: Toward a Corporeal Feminism* (Bloomington: Indiana University Press, 1994); Jon Simons, "Foucault's Mother," in Susan

Beckman, ed., *Feminist Interpretations of Michel Foucault* (University Park: Pennsylvania State University Press, 1996), 179–210.

30. On "the social force of the mother" see Cynthia Willett, *Maternal Ethics and Other Slave Moralities* (New York: Routledge, 1995), 65; and see Walter Benjamin, "Critique of Violence," trans. Edmund Jephcott, in Walter Benjamin *Selected Writings*, Markus Bullock and Michael W. Jennings, eds. (Cambridge, Mass.: Belknap Press of Harvard University Press, 1996), 236–52, where Benjamin associates weak messianic power with the caress of the air and with a contract, an agreement between generations, a claim of the past upon the present. I shall return to these, to Benjamin's mothers and to Niobe among them. For now, it might suffice that Benjamin offered his own attempt at self-analysis in the following terms: "It was as if I were determined never to form a united front with anyone, not even my own mother." Walter Benjamin, *Berlin Childhood Around 1900,* trans. Howard Eiland (Cambridge, Mass.: Belknap Press of Harvard University Press, 2006), 159).

31. Carolyn Dever, *Death and the Mother From Dickens to Freud: Victorian Fiction and the Anxiety of Origins* (Cambridge: Cambridge University Press,1998); *The Absent Mother in the Cultural Imagination: Missing, Presumed Dead,* Berit Åström, ed. (London: Palgrave Macmillan/Springer, 2017).

32. "A slave mother passed to her children the fact that they were 'not hers' " writes Barbara Johnson in her *Moses and Multiculturalism* (Berkeley: University of California Press, 2010), 42; and see Jennifer L. Morgan, "*Partus sequitur ventrem*: Law, Race, and Reproduction in Colonial Slavery," *Small Axe* 55 (March 2018): 1–17; and Yan Thomas, "Le 'ventre': Corps maternel, droit paternel," *Le Genre humain* 14, no. 1 (1986): 211–36.

33. Toni Morrison, *Beloved: A Novel* (New York: Vintage, 2004), 271, and consider the temporal and maternal complexities exposed by Octavia E. Butler in *Kindred* (Boston: Beacon, 2003).

34. Lee Edelman, *No Future: Queer Theory and the Death Drive* (Durham: Duke University Press, 2004); Jacques Derrida, "The Night Watch," trans. Pascale-Anne Brault and Michael Naas, in Andrew Mitchell and Sam Slote, eds., *Derrida and Joyce: Texts and Contexts* (Albany: State University of New York Press, 2013), 87–108.

35. Nancy Scheper-Hughes, *Death Without Weeping: The Violence of Everyday Life in Brazil* (Berkeley: University of California Press, 1992), 341.

36. On paleonymy, see Jacques Derrida, *Positions,* trans. Alan Bass (Chicago: University of Chicago Press, 1981), 71. Pertinent as it might be on some

prescriptive (or wishful) horizons, "parenting" would simply obfuscate what I am trying to describe, just as the paternal lexicon that dominates the tradition has done; and see Brian Duff, *The Parent as Citizen: A Democratic Dilemma* (Minneapolis: University of Minnesota Press, 2011).

37. On the way, Robert Meister's remarkable arguments were crucial as well, which set to work Donald Winnicott on the psychoanalyst as mother, as the recipient of aggression, as enemy or prototypical victim in an era that recognizes only past perpetrators, perpetrators as past. Robert Meister, *After Evil: A Politics of Human Rights* (New York: Columbia University Press, 2011).

38. Kittay, *Love's Labor*, 54n35.

39. Jeanne Lorraine Schroeder, *The Vestal and the Fasces: Hegel, Lacan, Property, and the Feminine* (Berkeley: University of California Press, 1998), 75.

40. I could not find a better term than *companionship*, which I borrow from the *hadith* I use as the epigraph to this book. It commonly translates the Arabic ṣuḥba, which does not have the connotation of breaking bread together (*cum-panis*), but covers a rich range of proximate and temporally extended togetherness from kinship to friendship and discipleship. Sara Ahmed proposes texts as companions (companions as texts?) and explains that "a companion text is a text whose company enabled you to proceed on a path less trodden" and "might spark a moment of revelation" or many "in the midst of an overwhelming proximity," a text that "might share a feeling or give you resources to make sense of something that had been beyond your grasp" or "prompt you to hesitate or to question the direction in which you are going" or else "give you a sense that in going the way you are going, you are not alone." Sara Ahmed, *Living a Feminist Life* (Durham: Duke University Press, 2017), 16. A mother-text.

41. Nicolas Abraham and Maria Torok, *The Shell and the Kernel: Renewals of Psychoanalysis,* with an introduction by Nicholas T. Rand, ed. and trans. (Chicago: University of Chicago Press, 1994), 96.

42. Saidiya Hartman, *Lose Your Mother: A Journey Along the Atlantic Slave Route* (New York: Farrar, Straus and Giroux, 2007), 91; on the mother as lost, see Jane Gallop, *Reading Lacan* (Ithaca: Cornell University Press, 1985), 148. And see Erich Fromm, *To Have or To Be?* (London: Continuum, 2008), where the mother only appears in a list of objects to be *had* (88).

43. Sara Ruddick, *Maternal Thinking: Toward a Politics of Peace* (Boston: Beacon, 1995), xii–xiii; 17, 22; I shall follow Ruddick, who herself acknowledges

Nancy Scheper-Hughes's work and includes "selection" as one of the tasks mothers might be confronted with (xiv).

44. Sarah Knott, *Mother Is a Verb: An Unconventional History* (New York: Picador, 2019).

45. Juliet Mitchell, *Fratriarchy: The Sibling Trauma and the Law of the Mother* (New York: Routledge, 2022); and see Amber Jacobs, *On Matricide: Myth, Psychoanalysis, and the Law of the Mother* (New York: Columbia University Press, 2007).

46. Willett, *Maternal Ethics*, 32; and see Young, *On Female Body Experience*, 52; on the pertinence of dance here and throughout, see Gil Anidjar, "D—ance," in Brad Evans and Chantal Mezza, eds., *State of Disappearance* (Montreal: McGill-Queens University Press, 2023), 210–30.

47. Sharon L. Snyder and David T. Mitchell, *Cultural Locations of Disability* (Chicago: University of Chicago Press, 2006), 8; and see, Cynthia Lewiecki-Wilson and Jen Cellio, *Disability and Mothering: Liminal Spaces of Embodied Knowledge* (Syracuse: Syracuse University Press, 2011).

48. Frederick Engels, *The Origin of the Family, Private Property and the State*, Eleanor Burke Leacock, ed. (New York: International,1972), 71.

49. Dotan Leshem, "The Ancient Art of Economics," *European Journal of the History of Economic Thought* 21, no. 2 (2014): 201–29.

50. Kittay, *Love's Labor*, 174.

51. My friend Avner Ofrath asked me to acknowledge that Marianne, as the French Republic, that strange *mère-patrie*, is clamorously called, decisively mothered me. So did my grandmother, I retorted (about whom, more later). As he consolidated his argument by way of Honoré Daumier's painting, *La République nourrit ses enfants et les instruit* (www.musee-orsay.fr/fr/oeuvres/la-republique-10865), my friend forced me to confront the formative role played by the *école maternelle* and other overt and covert mothers (Abbé Sieyès among them). Reluctant to give up on yet other maternal (matriarchal and matrilineal) constituencies, I half-grudgingly concede nevertheless.

52. Sarah Kofman, *Smothered Words*, trans. Madeleine Dobie (Evanston: Northwestern University Press, 1998).

53. Maurice Blanchot, *The Instant of My Death*, trans. Elizabeth Rottenberg (Stanford: Stanford University Press, 2000).

54. Martin Heidegger, *What Is Called Thinking*, trans. J. Glenn Gray (New York: HarperCollins, 1976), 48; and see Avital Ronell, *The Telephone Book:*

Technology, Schizophrenia, Electric Speech (Lincoln: University of Nebraska Press, 1989), 27.

55. Jacques Derrida, *The Animal That Therefore I Am*, trans. David Wills (New York: Fordham University Press, 2008).

56. Martin Heidegger, *Being and Time*, trans. John Macquarrie and Edward Robinson (San Francisco: Harper and Row, 1962), 275.

57. Luisa Muraro, *The Symbolic Order of the Mother*, trans. Francesca Novello (Albany: State University of New York Press, 2018), 6, 11; on mothers as undecidable text or context, see Anidjar, "Solicitude."

58. Ahmed, *Living a Feminist Life*, 14.

59. "The role of the mother was to generate the new citizen," writes Jacqueline Rose in *Mothers* (New York: Farrar, Straus & Giroux, 2018), 41; and see *inter alia*, Afsaneh Najmabadi,"The Erotic Vatan [Homeland] as Beloved and Mother: To Love, to Possess, and to Protect," *Comparative Studies in Society and History* 39, no. 3 (July 1997): 442–67; Firoozeh Kashani-Sabet, *Conceiving Citizens: Women and the Politics of Motherhood* (Oxford: Oxford University Press, 2011); Sumati Ramaswamy, *The Goddess and the Nation: Mapping Mother India* (Durham: Duke University Press, 2010); Beth Baron, *Egypt as a Woman: Nationalism, Gender and Politics* (Berkeley: University of California Press, 2005), Lisa Forman Cody, *Birthing the Nation: Sex, Science and the Conception of Eighteenth-Century Britons* (Oxford: Oxford University Press, 2005).

60. Friedrich Kittler, *Discourse Network 1800/1900*, trans. Michael Metteer and Chris Cullens (Stanford: Stanford University Press, 1990); Delphine Gardey, *Écrire, calculer, classer: Comment une révolution de papier a transformé les sociétés contemporaines (1800–1940)* (Paris: La découverte, 2008).

61. Thomas Paul Bonfiglio, *Mother Tongues and Nations: The Invention of the Native Speaker* (New York: de Gruyter, 2010).

1. MOTHER AND SLAVE

1. https://www.npr.org/sections/goatsandsoda/2016/07/30/487925796/it-takes-a-village-to-determine-the-origins-of-an-african-proverb. Accessed August 3, 2022.

2. Karuna Mantena, *Alibis of Empire: Henry Maine and the Ends of Liberal Imperialism* (Princeton: Princeton University Press, 2010), 80ff.

3. Jacqueline Rose, *Mothers* (New York: Farrar, Straus & Giroux, 2018), 154.

4. Daniel N. Stern and Nadia Bruschweiler-Stern, *The Birth of a Mother: How the Motherhood Experience Changes You Forever* (New York: Basic Books, 1998); and see Barbara Waterman, *The Birth of an Adoptive, Foster or Stepmother: Beyond Biological Mothering Attachment* (London: Jessica Kingsley, 2003). In *Birthing a Mother: The Surrogate Body and the Pregnant Self* (Berkeley: University of California Press, 2010), Elly Teman proposes that surrogacy must be understood as an act of birthing, that is to say, the act of a woman giving birth to an (other) mother.

5. Building on her notion of symbiosis, Margaret Mahler agrees with those who see in the mother "the auxiliary ego of the infant," which is to say that the mother is also "the symbiotic organizer—the midwife of individuation of psychological birth." Margaret S. Mahler, Fred Pine, and Anni Bergman, *The Psychological Birth of the Human Infant: Symbiosis and Individuation* (London: Karnac, 1985), 47. The mother *becomes*, in other words, she is *born again* as dual, as both mother and midwife.

6. What Eva Feder Kittay calls the "transparent self" of dependency workers, "a self through whom the needs of another are discerned, a self that, when it looks to gauge its own needs, sees first the needs of another . . . may seem too *servile* to be the autonomous agent of moral actions." Eva Feder Kittay, *Love's Labor: Essays on Women, Equality and Dependency* (New York: Routledge, 2020), 59. Note that Kittay locates the requirement and the obligation of the dependency worker in the realm of morality. The dependency worker is an individual in relation, indeed, interdependent, but she remains, grammatically and otherwise, one individual.

7. Elissa Marder elaborates on "the maternal function" throughout *The Mother in the Age of Mechanical Reproduction: Psychoanalysis, Photography, Deconstruction* (New York: Fordham University Press, 2012); the phrase, always in the singular, can also be found in the work of Julia Kristeva and others.

8. Sarah Blaffer Hrdy, *Mothers and Others: The Evolutionary Origins of Mutual Understanding* (Cambridge, Mass.: Belknap Press of Harvard University Press, 2009), ch. 3.

9. Rich distinguishes between "the potential relationship of any woman to her powers of reproduction and to children; and the institution, which aims at ensuring that that potential—and all women—shall remain under male control." Adrienne Rich, *Of Woman Born: Motherhood as Experience and Institution* (New York: Norton, 1986), 13.

10. Enid Balint, *Before I Was I: Psychoanalysis and the Imagination,* Juliet Mitchell and Michael Parsons, eds. (London: Free Association Books, 1993), 69.

11. Mantena, *Alibis of Empire,* 81.

12. Siri Hustvedt, *Mothers, Fathers, and Others: Essays* (New York: Simon and Schuster, 2021), 5; Anne Dufourmantelle refers to "ce territoire improbable qu'est le maternel" in *La sauvagerie maternelle* (Paris: Calmann-Lévy, 2011), whereas David Kishik reminds us that some cities, and first of all, New York City, may well be defined by their "motherlessness." New York would be "not a metropolis," Kishik writes, but "an *orbapolis* (orphan city) . . . its ego is split into a tale of two cities." David Kishik, *The Manhattan Project: A Theory of the City* (Stanford: Stanford University Press, 2015), 108. "The Great Mother" is a reference to Erich Neumann's important study, *The Great Mother: An Analysis of the Archetype,* trans. Ralph Manheim (Princeton: Princeton University Press, 2015).

13. Jacqueline Rose, *Mothers* (New York: Farrar, Straus & Giroux, 2018), 117; earlier in the book, Rose asks what became for me a crucial question: "Why are mothers not seen as having everything to contribute, by dint of being mothers, to our understanding and ordering of public, political space?" (Rose, *Mothers,* 17).

14. On the political as fraternal, see the distinct but congruent perspectives of Marc Shell, Carol Pateman, and Jacques Derrida, none of whom necessarily disagree with Juliet Mitchell, who considers "'fratriarchy,' the institution of brotherhood" (which must include, Mitchell adds, "the question of the individual sister in a social sisterhood") as "the neglected or ejected subject matter of psychoanalysis." Juliet Mitchell, *Fratriarchy: The Sibling Trauma and the Law of the Mother* (New York: Routledge, 2022), 187.

15. Jennifer Nash criticizes the "feminist birth industry," but the equation of mother and birth, the identification of "real" mother with birth mother, which obfuscates the temporalities of mothering, has a longer history. Jennifer C. Nash, *Birthing Black Mothers* (Durham: Duke University Press, 2021), 27.

16. Some of my language here is borrowed from Walter Benjamin's famous theses "On the Concept of History," trans. Harry Zohn, in Walter Benjamin, *Selected Writings 4,* Michael W. Jennings, ed. (Cambridge, Mass.: Belknap Press of Harvard University Press, 2003), 389–400.

17. James Baldwin, *The Fire Next Time* (New York: Vintage, 1993), 101; emphasis added.

18. Fred Moten, *Black and Blur* (Durham: Duke University Press, 2017), 177; Moten deploys this fantastic phrase while discussing Baldwin's *Just Above My Head*.

19. Maya Angelou, "The Mothering Blackness," in *The Complete Collected Poems of Maya Angelou* (New York: Random House, 1994), 22; Baldwin, for his part, may be said to have anticipated a "being maternal" that Fred Moten went on to describes as "indistinguishable from a *being material*," there were "enslavement—and the resistance to enslavement that is the performative essence of blackness (or, perhaps less controversially, the essence of black performance) is a *being maternal*." Fred Moten, *In the Break: Aesthetics of the Black Radical Tradition* (Minneapolis: University of Minnesota Press, 2003), 16; elsewhere Moten evokes a different materialism, at any rate, an impossible maternalism, given that "the impossible mother is always black, because blackness is impossible maternity." Moten, *Stolen Life* (Durham: Duke University Press, 2018), 238. As if maternality, as if motherhood, were ever *possible*.

20. Joy James, "The Womb of Western Theory: Trauma, Time Theft, and the Captive Maternal," *Carceral Notebooks* 12 (2016), available at www .thecarceral.org/cn12/14_Womb_of_Western_Theory.pdf.

21. Rose, *Mothers*, 32.

22. Benjamin, "On the Concept of History," 391.

23. Benjamin, 394.

24. Nash, *Birthing Black Mothers*, 4; on the "yoking" evoked here, see Moten, *Black and Blur*, xii.

25. Beverly Roberts Gaventa, *Our Mother Saint Paul* (Louisville, Ky.: Westminster John Knox, 2007).

26. Elizabeth A. Castelli, "Allegories of Hagar: Reading Galatians 4:21–31 with Postmodern Feminist Eyes," in Elizabeth Struthers Malbon and Edgar V. McKnight, eds., *The New Literary Criticism and the New Testament* (Sheffield: Sheffield Academic, 1994), 228–50; Amaryah Armstrong, "Of Flesh and Spirit: Race, Reproduction, and Sexual Difference in the Turn to Paul," *Journal for Cultural and Religious Theory* 16, no. 2 (Spring 2017): 126–41.

27. Augustine, *The City of God Against the Pagans*, trans. R. W. Dyson (Cambridge: Cambridge University Press, 1998).

28. Fethi Benslama, *Psychoanalysis and the Challenge of Islam*, trans. Robert Bononno (Minneapolis: University of Minnesota Press, 2009), 85.

29. Edward J. Bridge, "Female Slave vs. Female Slave: ʿamah and šiphah in the HB," *Journal of Hebrew Scriptures* 12 (2012): 1–21.

30. Neither the Septuagint (which uses *paidiskē*) nor the Vulgate (*ancilla*) register the different Hebrew terms in their translation of Genesis. In *Galatians,* Paul deploys derivatives of *doulos,* partly preserved in the modern *doula,* from which Kittay constructs her notion of *doulia*—"a term derived from the Greek word for service"—in *Love's Labor* (140). Peter Balla, "Paul's use of slavery imagery in the Hagar allegory," *In die Skriflig* 43, no. 1 (2009): 119–34. For more on the lexical and interpretive issues, see Savina J. Teubal, *Hagar the Egyptian: The Lost Tradition of the Matriarchs* (New York: Harper Collins, 1990), 49–70.

31. Some of the debates register in the bibliography I rely on, with regard to slavery; here I agree with Charles Mills (and many others) that "the racial contract" is a modern one, that race is a modern category whose deployment across social and epistemic fields is a recent one. Charles W. Mills, *The Racial Contract* (Ithaca: Cornell University Press, 1997), 63; and see Gil Anidjar, "The History of Race, the Race of History," *Jewish Quarterly Review* 105, no. 4 (Fall 2015): 515–21. For the purpose of the argument I make in this book, which is neither historical nor historicist, I read the dialectic of mother and slave as implicating, figuring or prefiguring, the problem of race. You might say that I have been reading *Kindred* a little too closely, that Octavia Butler's extraordinary rendering of the maternal contract is what occupies me throughout. However perverse, perverted, and perverting it might be, in any case, the role of the Bible in shaping racial arguments, about slavery and much else, along with its lingering effects, is important enough to try and reread the text in the manner I propose here, in the wake of others.

32. Eric Nelson, *The Hebrew Republic: Jewish Sources and the Transformation of European Political Thought* (Cambridge, Mass.: Harvard University Press, 2010).

33. The literature is obviously quite vast, but a good starting point can be found in the following exchange: Michael Walzer and Edward W. Said, "An Exchange: 'Exodus and Revolution,'" *Grand Street* 5, no. 4 (Summer 1986): 246–59; and there is more to be said about an emancipation that, at Sinai, becomes a new subjection, in this case, to divine rule and law.

34. Along with her archive, I extend Jennifer Nash's claim that "Black mothers become political currency when the category 'Black mother' comes to refer not to a form of relationally, a set of practices, a form of labor, or an embodied experience, but instead to a political category that is synonymous with pain" (Nash, *Birthing Black Mothers,* 4).

35. Augustine, *The City of God,* book 15, chapter 3, p. 637.

36. Benslama puts it too severely, therefore, when he writes that she is "kept out of the text, unreferenced" (Benslama, *Pyschoanalysis,* 103); and see Riffat Hassan, "Islamic Hagar and Her Family," in Phyllis Trible and Letty M. Russell, eds., *Hagar, Sarah, and Their Children: Jewish, Christian, and Muslim* Perspectives (Louisville, Ky.: Westminster John Knox, 2006), Kindle at 4155.

37. As Jennifer Glancy writes, "in a wide variety of Christian sources, the rhetoric of slavery represents the negative relationship of the human person to sin or the positive relationship of the Christian to God or to Christ" (Jennifer A. Glancy, *Slavery in Early Christianity* [Oxford: Oxford University Press, 2002], 10), furthermore, "because Paul subordinates the power of the flesh to the power of the spirit, generations of readers have been convinced that the hazards of mundane slavery must pale in comparison to the evils of spiritual bondage" (38). On Christianity and its others, from Hagar onward, see, e.g., Fergus Millar, "Hagar, Ishmael, Josephus and the Origins of Islam," *Journal of Jewish Studies* 44 (1993): 23–45, and, for a different genealogy, Gil Anidjar, *The Jew, the Arab: A History of the Enemy* (Stanford: Stanford University Press, 2003).

38. Tikva Frymer-Kensky, *Reading the Women of the Bible* (New York: Schocken, 2002), 233; and see Yvonne Sherwood, "Hagar and Ishmael: The Reception of Expulsion," *Interpretation: A Journal of Bible and Theology* 68, no. 3 (2014): 286–304.

39. Adele Reinhartz and Miriam-Simma Walfish, "Conflict and Coexistence in Jewish Interpretation," in Trible and Russell, *Hagar, Sarah, and Their Children,* Kindle at 3230.

40. Delores S. Williams, *Sisters in the Wilderness: The Challenge of Womanist God-Talk* (Ossining, N.Y.: Orbis, 2013), 3.

41. John W. Waters, "Who Was Hagar?" in Cain Hope Felder, ed., *Stony the Road We Trod: African American Biblical Interpretation* (Minneapolis: Fortress, 1991), 187–205; Teubal, *Hagar the Egyptian*; Stephanie Buckhanon Crowder, *When Momma Speaks: The Bible and Motherhood from a Womanist Perspective* (Louisville, Ky.: Westminster John Knox, 2016); Janet Gabler-Hover, *Dreaming Black/Writing White: The Hagar Myth in American Cultural History* (Lexington: University of Kentucky Press, 2000); Ruth Tsoffar, *Life in Citations: Biblical Narratives and Contemporary Hebrew Culture* (New York: Routledge, 2020); Nyasha Junior, *Reimagining Hagar: Blackness and Bible* (Oxford: Oxford University Press, 2019); Armstrong, "Of Flesh and Spirit."

42. Hortense J. Spillers, "Mama's Baby, Papa's Maybe: An American Grammar Book," in Spillers, *Black, White, and in Color: Essays on American Literature and Culture* (Chicago: University of Chicago Press, 2003), 203–29; "the *longue durée* of slavery" is Jennifer Nash's phrase (Nash, *Birthing Black Mothers*, 17).
43. Spillers, "Mama's Baby," 228.
44. On "othermothers," see Patricia Hill Collins, "The Meaning of Motherhood in Black Culture and Black Mother/Daughter Relationships," *SAGE* 4, no. 2 (Fall 1987): 4; Nancy Scheper-Hughes reports on Brazil's *comadres*, com-others or godmothers, those "midwives, healing women, and praying women, those entrusted with the well-being of children and other family members." Nancy Scheper-Hughes, *Death Without Weeping: The Violence of Everyday Life in Brazil* (Berkeley: University of California Press, 1992), 559.
45. Spillers, "Mama's Baby," 224.
46. Moten, *In the Break*, 16.
47. Nash, *Birthing Black Mothers*, 17.
48. Isaac D. Balbus, *Marxism and Domination: A Neo-Hegelian, Feminist, Psychoanalytic Theory of Sexual, Political, and Technological Liberation* (Princeton: Princeton University Press, 1982).
49. "God is the originary withdrawal of the father," writes Fethi Benslama in *Psychoanalysis*, 87; and see Balbus.
50. Simone de Beauvoir, *The Second Sex*, trans. Constance Borde and Sheila Malovany-Chevalier (New York: Vintage, 2011), 568.
51. Vicky Shiran, "Decoding Power, Creating a New World" [in Hebrew] *Panim* 99 (2002): 16.
52. Jessica Benjamin, *The Bonds of Love: Psychoanalysis, Feminism, and the Problem of Domination* (New York: Pantheon, 1988), 82.
53. Benjamin, *The Bonds of Love*, 82.
54. The title of this section was inspired by Susan Buck-Morss, *Hegel, Haiti, and Universal History* (Pittsburgh: University of Pittsburgh Press, 2009); my argument being that, in addition to the news media, Hegel was always already reading the Bible.
55. On the technological, specifically, prosthetic dimension of the maternal body—beginning with Pandora—and "the prosthetic maternal," see Marder, *The Mother in the Age of Mechanical Reproduction*, 89 and *passim*.
56. Zakiyyah Iman Jackson, *Becoming Human: Matter and Meaning in an Antiblack World* (New York: New York University Press, 2020), 39, 90; Jackson writes of "the state of occupying two distinct and seemingly contradictory human and object worlds simultaneously" (116).

57. "The Hebrew verb *bānā* is used to denote 'the building of a family, people, dynasty or individual, and to describe the creation of the world in theological contexts.'" Cynthia R. Chapman, *The House of the Mother: The Social Roles of Maternal Kin in Biblical Hebrew Narrative and Poetry* (New Haven: Yale University Press, 2016), 150. The words for "son" or "daughter" are considered derivatives of that verb, which has cognates in Ugaritic and Akkadian, and means "'to build,' 'to engender,' as in a father engendering a son, and 'to create'" (Chapman). Ruth Tsoffar offers the apt neologism "sonned": Sarah "desires to be 'sonned,' to become a mother through Hagar" (Tsoffar, *Life in Citations*, 101); Sarah wants to have a son, to build a house, to establish herself, and she uses her slave Hagar to do so.

58. Trible and Russell, *Hagar, Sarah, and Their Children*, Kindle at 2898.

59. Orlando Patterson, whose understanding of slavery as social death has been hugely influential, also proposed that the slave is an exile, "an external exile" (originally an outsider) or "an internal exile . . . deprived of all claims to community." Orlando Patterson, *Slavery and Social Death: A Comparative Study* (Cambridge, Mass.: Harvard University Press, 1982), 44; and see John Bodel and Walter Scheidel, eds., *On Human Bondage: After Slavery and Social Death* (Malden, Mass.: Wiley Blackwell, 2017).

60. Gerard Aching, "The Slave's Work: Reading Slavery Through Hegel's Master-Slave Dialectic," *PMLA* 127, no. 4 (2012): 916; in this essay, Aching attends to "the lofty servitude of friendship," to the significance of "a higher form of bondage," which is "the affection that binds slaves to their friends" (916). Aching mentions Margaret Garner, the mother who inspired Toni Morrison's *Beloved*, suggesting that the "lofty servitude" and the binding affection of which Aching speaks, certainly involved mothers and children, mothers and mothers, mothers and slaves.

61. Tsoffar, *Life in Citations*, 102–3; and see J. Cheryl Exum, *Art as Biblical Commentary: Visual Criticism from Hagar the Wife of Abraham to Mary the Mother of Jesus* (London: T&T Clark, 2019).

62. After Hegel or against him, and since Carla Lonzi's 1970 "Let's Spit on Hegel" at least, the dialectic of master and slave has occupied many a feminist mind, focusing on men and women, husbands and wives, as well as on mother and child. Jessica Benjamin made clear that Hegel *should* have been reading mothers as well, indeed, mothers and slaves. Jessica Benjamin, *The Bonds of Love: Psychoanalysis, Feminism, and the Problem of Domination* (New York: Pantheon, 1988), especially ch. 2. Between these lines, the mother emerges as both dominant and subservient, as both master and

slave. I myself attend to that pairing, mother and slave, not, again, in order to "return to Hegel" but rather to return to the Bible, and to turn toward an absence, one that structures or governs the relation between two mothers (two mothers at least) and, more precisely, between mother and slave. The complex pairing also speaks to the oscillating rapport between mother and child, as it must, in which the Child—His Majesty the Baby—must be acknowledged as a concrete figure of domination, *pace* Dorothy Dinnerstein, as a being who subjects the mother to needs and desires, to will and to demands. Dorothy Dinnerstein, *The Mermaid and the Minotaur: Sexual Arrangements and Human Malaise* (New York: Other, 1999).

63. Georg Wilhelm Friedrich Hegel, *Phenomenology of Spirit,* trans. Terry Pinkard (Cambridge: Cambridge University Press, 2018), 114.

64. Benslama, *Psychoanalysis,* 83; translation altered following the French *souveraine* (which the English inexplicably renders "mistress"), a matter of significance, as I will be arguing.

65. Tsoffar, *Life in Citations*, 103; Amaryah Armstrong aptly writes here of "the circulation of sovereignty via the economy of kinship" ("Of Flesh and Spirit," 128).

66. Benslama, *Psychoanalysis and the Challenge of Islam,* 81.

67. Hegel, *Phenomenology of Spirit*, trans. Pinkard, 109, turning Hegel's masculine to feminine.

68. Benslama, *Psychoanalysis and the Challenge of Islam,* 81–82.

69. Hegel, *Phenomenology of Spirit,* 114.

70. Both Teubal, *Hagar the Egyptian* and Williams, *Sisters in the Wilderness,* underscore the importance of the revelation, Hagar as prophetess.

71. Moten, *In the Break*, 12.

72. Commentaries are sparse on the change of terms, with some deeming *amah* worse off than *shifḥah,* others the reverse; see, e.g., Phyllis Trible, *Texts of Terror* (Philadelphia: Fortress, 1984), 21. Questions of inclusion and exclusion are found within both words, with *shifḥah* possibly related to *mishpaḥah* (translated "family" or "tribe") and *amah* evoking a maternal function. Yet the term *Hebrew* is often associated with *amah,* which suggests a more intimate proximity. I shall return to *omenet* and to the contract.

73. The association of *ummah* and *'umm* is etymologically dubious (Louis Massignon's claim notwithstanding), but, again, the words obviously resonate; see Salim Daccache, "La notion d'Umma dans Is Goran," *Annates de philosophie* 3 (1982): 11; Maysam J. Al Faruqi, "*Umma*: The Orientalists and

the Qur'ānic Concept of Identity," *Journal of Islamic Studies* 16, no. 1 (2005): 23.

74. Armstrong, "Of Flesh and Spirit," 138.

75. Jennifer A. Glancy, "The Mistress-Slave Dialectic: Paradoxes of Slavery in Three LXX Narratives," *Journal of the Study of the Old Testament* 72 (1996): 71–87.

76. Whether these terms are "Greek," or "ancient Greek," in the all-too accepted sense of the phrase, is exactingly interrogated by Stathis Gourgouris in *Nothing Sacred* (New York: Columbia University Press, 2024).

77. The TV series *Atlanta* has a remarkable episode entitled "Trini 2 de Bone" (season 3, episode 7), which illustrates the matter better than I could. And see, e.g., Jacqueline Jones, *Labor of Love, Labor of Sorrow: Black Women, Work, and the Family, from Slavery to the Present* (New York: Perseus, 2010).

78. "Because Sarah had a younger, fertile Egyptian slave woman in her household at the time of Isaac's birth, one might assume that Hagar would become Isaac's wet nurse. Indeed, if breast milk were simply a substance of nourishment, Hagar would be an ideal solution to the problem of a ninety-year-old mother who needs to provide for her infant" (Chapman, *The House of the Mother*, 138). Chapman follows the biblical text, which seems purposefully to mention that Sarah herself nursed Isaac, although the possibility that Hagar did serve as a wet nurse to Isaac remains open (140). But the significance of Hagar's role, of the maternal functions she could and did play, is hardly restricted to nursing, obviously.

79. Benslama, who otherwise seems to know better (186), insists on collapsing the maternal and the feminine, writing here of "two conflicting figures of the feminine" (*Psychoanalysis and the Challenge of Islam*, 98). Hagar remains for him the figure of "the other woman" (110), not "the other mother." It is therefore "woman" who is, for him, "double" (110). By the same token, when Hagar, the enslaved woman, is denied her maternality, when she "does not acquire the position of 'Her Highness the Mother,'" Benslama folds her back onto her womanhood, rather than onto her enslavement (110). Benslama goes on to revisit the matter of the "Between-Two-Women in Psychoanalysis" (117), as he attends to Moses, and here too, it is of woman that he speaks, and more precisely of a (unique) mother who is opposed to a (foreign) woman (116). I shall have more to say about Moses in the next chapters.

80. Cynthia Willett, *Maternal Ethics and Other Slave Moralities* (New York: Routledge, 1995), 68; Adrienne Rich famously writes that "the physical and psychic weight of responsibility" on the mother is "the heaviest of social

burdens." Still, Rich continues, if "it cannot be compared with slavery or sweated labor"—a comparison Rich is herself making here—it is only because of emotions, "because the emotional bonds between a woman and her children make her vulnerable in ways which the forced laborer does not know; he can hate and fear his boss or master, loathe the toil; dream of revolt or of becoming a boss; the woman with children is a prey to far more complicated, subversive feelings" (Rich, *Of Woman Born,* 52). I wonder. Rich is certainly right that one person should not be "held accountable for her children's health, the clothes they wear, their behavior at school, their intelligence and general development" and much more (53). Motherhood is work, it is "essential labor," as Garbes writes. Angela Garbes, *Essential Labor: Mothering as Social Change* (New York: HarperCollins, 2022). The work, the dependency work (in Eva Feder Kittay's phrase), must be performed, responsibilities must be shouldered (preferably, collectively). Not only by women but certainly by mothers. The weight of responsibility may, moreover, be made lighter by being shared, but it remains a call to service, to servitude even, that must be answered. Thus, mother and slave.

81. I pursue the matter differently than Willett, but her rich formulation resonates powerfully as a reading of Hegel and of motherhood in its relation to service and servitude. "If intersubjectivity emerges earlier than those struggles for domination that divide the world into masters and slaves, might it not emerge already in the relation between mothers and other caregivers and their children?" (Willett, *Maternal Ethics*, 63); and see her discussion of Levinas and "the asymmetry of service" (84). In her compelling reading of Hegel—and of Frederick Douglass—Willett identifies a recurring "negation of the sphere of the mother" (170). She is, I think, most invested in that which distinguishes the mother from the slave and, more generally, intersubjectivity from domination and struggle.

82. Armstrong, "Of Flesh and Spirit," 141.

83. I borrow and alter Fethi Benslama's formulation, which has "the same woman split between two poles of the feminine" (Benslama, *Psychoanalysis and the Challenge of Islam*, 123).

84. "Monotheism," writes Benslama in a clarifying moment, "has been built on the writing of the originary rent between two principles embodied by two maternal figures" (89). It might be recalled that, in *Moses and Monotheism* (the more faithful translation of the book title being "The Man Moses and the Monotheistic Religion"), Freud had argued there were two men called Moses.

2. OF MOTHERS BORN

1. Jacqueline Rose, *Mothers* (New York: Farrar, Straus & Giroux, 2018), 157.
2. See, e.g., Shuli Barzilai, *Lacan and the Matter of Origins* (Stanford: Stanford University Press, 1999), a compelling reading of Lacan and the vanishing maternal imago in his work, his "reassignment of terminology or functions associated with the mother" (111).
3. Everything is as if the historical moment described by Friedrich Kittler had not quite passed. As Kittler writes, "The Mother, or source of all discourse, was at the same time the abyss into which everything vanished, only to emerge as pure Spirit and Voice." Friedrich Kittler, *Discourse Networks 1800/1900*, trans. Michael Metteer and Chris Cullens (Stanford: Stanford University Press, 1990), 54; contrary to this tendency, I do not understand mothers as sources, origins or foundations, nor as "mother-centered beginnings." And see Sarah Blaffer Hrdy, *Mothers and Others: The Evolutionary Origins of Mutual Understanding* (Cambridge, Mass.: Belknap Press of Harvard University Press, 2009): "I need to begin at the beginning, with mothers" (68).
4. Jennifer C. Nash, *Birthing Black Mothers* (Durham: Duke University Press, 2021), 27.
5. "We must surely contend with the notion that motherhood produces something new" writes Lisa Baraitser, *Maternal Encounters: The Ethics of Interruption* (New York: Routledge, 2009), 6.
6. "Under patriarchal institutions of motherhood," writes Willett, "maternal labor may indeed be reduced to the alienating rhythms of flat tonalities of mechanistic repetition." Cynthia Willett, *Maternal Ethics and Other Slave Moralities* (New York: Routledge, 1995), 40. But the repetitive demands of motherhood do not have to fall on one lone woman to be thereby accurately described, if to different rhythms. There are reasons why "the infant threatens to exhaust and alienate" (43). The infant, not just the patriarchy.
7. Honaida Ghanem, "Between Holy Mary and Umna el-Ghula: Reflections on an Anxious Motherhood," in Erella Shadmi, ed., *The Legacy of Mothers: Matriarchies and the Gift Economy as Post-Capitalist Alternatives* (Toronto: Inanna, 2021), 47.
8. "By giving birth, [a mother] touches her mother, she becomes her, she is her, they are the same continuity differentiating itself," writes Julia Kristeva, *Desire in Language: A Semiotic Approach to Literature and Art*, trans.

Thomas Gora, Alice Jardine, and Leon Roudiez (New York: Columbia University Press, 1980), 239; trans. modified; and see Michelle Boulous Walker, *Philosophy and the Maternal Body: Reading Silence* (New York: Routledge, 1998).

9. Luisa Muraro, *The Symbolic Order of the Mother,* trans. Francesca Novello (Albany: State University of New York Press, 2018), 52; in a chapter entitled "Or the One in Her Place," Muraro refers to "the well-known and wonderful fact according to which the biological mother can be replaced by other figures"—note the plural form—"without causing the loss of the fundamental characteristics of the mother's relationship with her child" (51). Muraro reinscribes on the next page "our ability to accept substitutes for the mother" (53), "a sequence of mothers" (57).

10. Rose, *Mothers,* 124.

11. Jacques Derrida, *Hospitalité,* vol. 1: *Séminaire (1995-1996),* Pascale-Anne Brault and Peggy Kamuf, eds. (Paris: Seuil, 2021); Andrew Parker, *The Theorist's Mother* (Durham: Duke University Press, 2012); Gil Anidjar, "Solicitude," in *Derrida Today* 16, no. 1 (2023), 3–19. On reproduction, the literature is vast, but I have learned most from Mary O'Brien, *The Politics of Reproduction* (London: Routledge & Kegan Paul, 1981); Faye D Ginsburg and Rayna Rapp, eds., *Conceiving the New World Order: The Global Politics of Reproduction* (Berkeley: University of California Press, 1995); Alys Eve Weynbaum, *Wayward Reproductions: Genealogies of Race and Nation in Transatlantic Modern Thought* (Durham: Duke University Press, 2004); Nick Hopwood, Rebecca Flemming, and Lauren Kassell, eds., *Reproduction: Antiquity to the Present Day* (Cambridge: Cambridge University Press, 2018).

12. Janet Adelman, *Suffocating Mothers: Fantasies of Maternal Origin in Shakespeare's Plays,* Hamlet *to* The Tempest (New York: Routledge, 1992), 5; and compare with Kristeva, who writes that "the maternal body is the place of a splitting" (Kristeva, *Desire in Language,* 238).

13. Rita Segato, *The Critique of Coloniality: Eight Essays,* trans. Ramsey McGlazer (New York: Routledge, 2022), 138; Shelley M. Park, *Mothering Queerly, Queering Motherhood: Resisting Monomaternalism in Adoptive, Lesbian, Blended, and Polygamous Families* (Albany: State University of New York Press, 2013).

14. Segato, *The Critique of Coloniality,* 136; Segato strangely confines her argument to colonial Brazil (the essay was originally published as *O édipo brasileiro*), although there is the suggestion of a more generalized condition, as we shall see.

15. Lee Edelman, in *No Future: Queer Theory and the Death Drive* (Durham: Duke University Press, 2004), makes this argument most forcefully.

16. Segato, *The Critique of Coloniality*, 141.

17. Carol Pateman, *The Sexual Contract* (Stanford: Stanford University Press, 1988); Charles W. Mills, *The Racial Contract* (Ithaca: Cornell University Press, 1997).

18. Virginia Held, "Non-contractual Society: A Feminist View," *Canadian Journal of Philosophy* 13, sup 1 (1987): 111–37; Held has excellent reasons to understand the social contract as predicated on "economic man," and she proposes "mothering" as an alternative to "contracting," the mother-child relation, a primary relation, as "an alternative to the conception of economic man in contractual relations" (116), which I obviously found compelling. And even though she writes that "we should look to the relation between mothering person and child for suggestions on how better to describe such society as we now have" (125), she remains prescriptive (or imaginative) and future oriented. Held also insists on "the family," on the creation of "autonomous persons," and conceives of the mother (or mothering person) in terms of permanence and nonreplaceability, of caring and concern, all of which belongs to the domestic sphere or to the realm of morality.

19. Pateman, *The Sexual Contract*, 8; Mills, *The Racial Contract*, 16.

20. Juliet Mitchell, who foregrounds the lesser studied social, horizontal axis, sees the mother's role, the mother's law, as formative for siblings' relations. On this basis, Mitchell distinguishes two mothers in one, namely, "the mother of the family" and "the mother of the social." Juliet Mitchell, *Fratriarchy: The Sibling Trauma and the Law of the Mother* (New York: Routledge, 2022), 43.

21. Segato, *The Critique of Coloniality*, 148.

22. Segato, 150.

23. Segato, 151.

24. Ernst Kantorowicz, *The King's Two Bodies: A Study in Medieval Political Theology* (Princeton: Princeton University Press, 2016); Segato mentions Kantorowicz but does not adopt his phrasing (Segato, *The Critique of Coloniality*, 144). I keep my scholarly allegiances but nonetheless decided to change the original title of this lecture, from "The Mother's Two Bodies," and return instead, with all due respect, to Adrienne Rich; hence, "Of Mothers Born."

25. The *fort/da* game, which Jay Watson brilliantly recasts as "little Ernst's crash course in mothering," is narrated by Freud in *Beyond the Pleasure Principle*. It has generated extensive commentary, much of it is reviewed by Watson. Jay Watson, "Guys and Dolls: Exploratory Repetition and Maternal Subjectivity in the Fort/Da Game," *American Imago* 52, no. 4 (Winter 1995): 463–503; Freud does refer briefly to matriarchy in *Moses and Monotheism*.

26. Sigmund Freud, "The Theme of the Three Caskets," trans. C. J. M. Hubback, in *The Standard Edition of the Complete Psychological Works of Sigmund Freud (1911-1913)*, James Strachey, ed (London: Hogarth and the Institute of Psycho-Analysis, 1958), 7:301; and see Gilles Deleuze, "Coldness and Cruelty," trans. Jean McNeil, in *Masochism* (New York: Zone, 1991). I am grateful to Tracy McNulty for these references and for reminding me of the three caskets/three mothers.

27. I borrow this version from Barbara Johnson in her *Moses and Multiculturalism* (Berkeley: University of California Press, 2010), 74; Johnson attends to slave mothers and registers as well "Moses's complicated relations with his two mothers" (39). Johnson also writes that there were "two major ways that mothers affected, and were affected by, chattel slavery: the division between the birth mother and the owner of a child and the fact that a child 'follows the condition of the mother'" (42). I have already quoted the rest of that paragraph: "A slave mother passed to her children the fact that they were 'not hers.'"

28. One example from Winnicott should suffice, who writes that "the care of a new-born infant is a whole-time job, and . . . it can be done well by only one person." Donald Winnicott, *The Child, the Family and the Outside World* (Cambridge, Mass: Perseus, 1987), 24, and see 88; at the same time, it is again striking that Winnicott—who understood psychoanalysts as functioning mothers, as occupying the position of substitute mothers—described himself as "*an only child with multiple mothers*"; quoted in Adam Phillips, *Winnicott* (New York: Fontana, 1988), 28; emphasis added. Winnicott complained that his father left him "too much to all my mothers," among whom he counts, as Phillips explains, "not only two older sisters but also a nanny and a governess" (28). Needless to say, Phillips—and Winnicott—will continue, like countless others, to write mostly of "the mother" in the singular ("Ironically, Winnicott's mother is a more shadowy figure" [28]). Juliet Mitchell points to another instance—the sibling

trauma—whereby Winnicott's clinical acumen informed his descriptions
but failed to alter the theorization (Mitchell, *Fratriarchy*, 95ff.).

29. Adrienne Rich, *Of Woman Born: Motherhood as Experience and Institution* (New York: Norton, 1986), 253.

30. Jim Swan noted "the remarkable circumstance that Freud had, in effect, *two* mothers," but restricts the pertinence of that fact as a "part of the whole white European, bourgeois, child-rearing pattern of hiring nurses to care for infants." Jim Swan, "Mater and Nannie: Freud's Two Mothers and the Discovery of the Oedipus Complex," *American Imago* 31 (1974): 35. Less than politically correct, Swan does acknowledge the parallel with "the American slave-holding south where white infants were nursed by black Mammies and grew up into a culture that idealized white women" (36).

31. Prophecy Coles, *The Shadow of the Second Mother: Nurses and Nannies in Theories of Infant Development* (London: Routledge, 2015).

32. Shuli Barzilai offers a rich review and corrective to the literature on the stepmother in her "Reading 'Snow White': The Mother's Story," *Signs* 15, no. 3 (Spring 1990): 515–34.

33. Silvia Federici, *Caliban and the Witch: Women, the Body and Primitive Accumulation* (New York: Autonomedia, 2004); and see Martha E. Gimenez, *Marx, Women, and Capitalist Social Reproduction: Marxist Feminist Essays* (Leiden: Brill, 2019).

34. Rich, *Of Woman Born,* 254.

35. I shall follow Fred Moten again and point out that "there's a tangent I want to go off on right now about the tension between midwifery/maternity and sovereignty but I will refrain"—for the time being, that is. Fred Moten, *Stolen Life* (Durham: Duke University Press, 2018), 232.

36. This is Joel Whitebook's phrase, commenting on Freud's failure to discuss the patriarch Abraham as well as his collaborator Karl Abraham. Joel Whitebook, *Freud: An Intellectual Biography* (Cambridge: Cambridge University Press, 2017), 451.

37. Johnson, *Moses and Multiculturalism*, 43; whether this is the command, or the demand, of the God of Abraham, I could not say, even if Johnson's formulation has indubitable explanatory appeal: "having no other gods before the God of Abraham requires that one have no other mothers before the one whose condition one has to share" (43). Johnson does prevaricate on her own monomaternalism: "one of the most uncanny attractions of Egypt is thus the idea that European culture might have a double origin. It might have two mothers, in effect" (50).

38. Many witches were midwives, a profession that came to be monopolized by men in the wake of the witch hunt. Incidentally, as Silvia Federici describes, the witch was also "the servant, the slave" of the Devil (Federici, *Caliban and the Witch*, 187); Prophecy Coles traces a history of "privileged" children who were cared for by "nurses" (which she does grant were "delegated mothers," indeed, *second mothers*). Coles acknowledges Freud's "preoccupation" with individuals who had two mothers. She also alludes to the significance of slavery but glosses over it quite quickly, and she does not extend her analysis to the larger structure, or infrastructure, that occupies me (Coles, *The Shadow of the Second Mother*, especially 102–4).

39. Whitebook, *Freud: An Intellectual Biography*, 42–43; Whitebook also refers to Swan, "Mater and Nannie," in which Swan proposes, "in a relatively oversimplified manner of speaking," that "the early split between good, pure, nurturing mother and ugly, sexual, humiliating mother gets redistributed in the later relationship between pure mother and humiliating father" (33).

40. Sarah Kofman, *The Childhood of Art: An Interpretation of Freud's Aesthetics*, trans. Winnifred Woodhull (New York: Columbia University Press, 1988), 82; and see Kofman's own harrowing story of two mothers in her *Rue Ordener, Rue Labat*, trans. Ann Smock (Lincoln: University of Nebraska Press, 1996); Jonathan Boyarin, *Jewish Families* (New Brunswick: Rutgers University Press, 2013), 137–38.

41. Massimo Recalcati devotes a few pages to the famous trial of two mothers, where King Solomon renders his famous judgment. Massimo Recalcati, *The Mother's Hands: Desire, Fantasy and the Inheritance of the Maternal*, trans. Alice Kilgarriff (Cambridge: Polity, 2019). For Recalcati, "the two mothers are not *really* two mothers, but demonstrate a splitting in the experience of motherhood" (75); of such "two faces," though, Recalcati accordingly grants "authenticity" only to the mother who knows how to renounce and free the child "as Abraham and Sarah did with Isaac . . ." (78).

42. David's mother is not mentioned in the biblical narrative, but see Ruth Kara-Ivanov Kaniel, *Holiness and Transgression: Mothers of the Messiah in the Jewish Myth,* trans. Eugene D. Matanky with Ruth Kara-Ivanov Kaniel (Boston: Academic Studies Press, 2017), 11, 77; the midrash in question is the *Yalkhut ha-Makhiri*, a fourteenth-century collection of likely earlier material (76). Kara-Ivanov Kaniel briefly elaborates on what she calls "the absent mother and the excessive mother" (80), attributing to the exegete

the implicit notion that "excess and duality are the essence of the maternal experience" (82).

43. Reiko Ohnuma, *Ties That Bind: Maternal Imagery and Discourse in Indian Buddhism* (Oxford: Oxford University Press, 2012), 66.

44. Ohnuma, 66.

45. Ohnuma, 67.

46. Ohnuma, 69.

47. Ohnuma, 66. One can identify the resemblance between Māyā and Mary, mother of Jesus, which Ohnuma explores as well.

48. Ohnuma, *Ties That Bind*, 29; later Ohnuma writes that sons are advised "to recognize *many mothers* rather than none" (31); what emerges here is a generalized maternality, in which a son is advised "to view *all women* as his mothers" (32), "to reflect on the fact that *all* sentient beings, at one time or another, have served as his mother and have similarly suffered for his welfare" (33).

49. Ohnuma, 57.

50. Quoted in Elisheva Baumgarten, *Mothers and Children: Jewish Family Life in Medieval Europe* (Princeton: Princeton University Press, 2004), 159.

51. Carl Schmitt, *Hamlet or Hecuba: The Intrusion of the Time Into the Play*, trans. David Pan and Jennifer R. Rust (Candor, N.Y.: Telos, 2009), 96; Schmitt also underscores the significance of Walter Benjamin's title (191).

52. Schmitt identifies the crimes of Mary Stuart, the historical figure he sees as governing the play. Schmitt writes that "Mary Stuart is still for us something other and more than Hecuba" (177); yet, as Jill Frank pointed out to me, Hecuba is certainly paradigmatic, otherwise paradigmatic, being both queen and slave, a queen become slave. Rachel Bowlby adds that Hecuba is "the acknowledged mothers of . . . hundred sons and daughters." Rachel Bowlby, *Freudian Mythologies: Greek Tragedy and Modern Identities* (Oxford: Oxford University Press, 2007), 97.

53. Adelman, *Suffocating Mothers*, 11; after Campbell and Farred, we might ask whether there is comedy in the tragedy that is history, whether the maternal is not quite precisely where the comic self—"I disown myself"— might emerge. Timothy Campbell and Grant Farred, *The Comic Self: Toward Dispossession* (Minneapolis: University of Minnesota Press, 2023), 17; and see their reading of *Hamlet* sans Gertrude (101–8). Or comic selves.

54. "For Lacan, Hamlet's problem is Gertrude . . . Lacan emphasizes Hamlet's subjection to the desire of the mother." Julia Reinhard Lupton and Kenneth Reinhard, *After Oedipus: Shakespeare in Psychoanalysis* (Ithaca: Cornell

University Press, 1993), 74, whereas Eliot "claimed that the major issue of the play is 'the effect of a mother's guilt upon her son'" (112).

55. "We would emphasize that, although Ophelia appears as the means of Hamlet's separation from his mother through the acquisition of a new object . . . Ophelia is nonetheless continually linked in the play to Gertrude, and to Gertrude not as object of incestuous desire but as maternal Other of demand" (Lupton and Reinhard, *After Oedipus,* 81); Lupton and Reinhard also elaborate on Niobe, underscoring the association of Antigone to Niobe (111, 126).

56. Adelman, *Suffocating Mothers,* 18; "the killing attaches itself irrevocably to Gertrude," Adelman goes on, "she becomes the active murderer" (25, and see 30).

57. Adelman, 29; and this is "why the confrontation of Hamlet with Gertrude in the closet scene seems much more central, much more vivid, than any confrontation between Hamlet and Claudius" (31).

58. *Hamlet* 4.3; quoted in Adelman, *Suffocating Mothers,* 28.

59. Lupton and Reinhard, *After Oedipus,* 48.

60. Adelman, *Suffocating Mothers,* 30.

61. Adelman, 34.

62. "It scarcely needs saying that our understanding of the story of Oedipus is enriched when we know the story of Jocasta, and vice versa," writes Natalie Haynes in *Pandora's Jar: Women in the Greek Myths* (London: Picador, 2020), 51.

63. Upon which, Jean-Joseph Goux comments: "And Jung, seeking the meaning of this dangerous creature, was right to look to the mother, to the dark, enveloping, stifling mother who binds and captivates her son, holds him back, traps him in the numberless coils of her reptilian attachment." Jean-Joseph Goux, *Oedipus, Philosopher,* trans. Catherine Porter (Stanford: Stanford University Press, 1993), 26.

64. Carl G. Jung, *Symbols of Transformation: An Analysis of the Prelude to a Case of Schizophrenia,* trans. R. F. C. Hull (Princeton: Bollingen/Princeton University Press, 1976), 181; Jung was, nevertheless, interested in "the dual mother," which he thought a motif that could be "replaced by the motif of dual birth" (321). Indeed, "the dual-mother motif suggests the idea of a dual birth. One of the mothers is the real, human mother, the other is the symbolical mother" (322).

65. Mary G. Dietz, "Citizenship with a Feminist Face: The Problem with Maternal Thinking," *Political Theory* 13, no. 1 (February 1985): 27.

66. Eric Dugdale, "Who Named Me? Identity and Status in Sophocles' 'Oedipus Tyrannus," *American Journal of Philology* 136, no. 3 (Fall 2015): 421–45.

67. Hendrika C. Freud, *Men and Mothers: The Lifelong Struggle of Sons and Their Mothers,* trans. Marjolijn de Jager (London: Karnac, 2013), xxii.

68. "Merope emerges only as an almost abstracted source of fear," writes Rachel Bowlby (*Freudian Mythologies*, 180). Bowlby is the only reader I found who compares Jocasta and Merope and relates to Merope in her own right at any length. Bowlby does not seem to register how singular and remarkable her treatment is of these figures.

69. Tina Chanter, *Whose Antigone? The Tragic Marginalization of Slavery* (Albany: State University of New York Press, 2011), xxxvii.

70. Segato, *The Critique of Coloniality*, 138; Karen Carducci provides a quick but fascinating reception history of the character of Jocasta. Karen Carducci, "Redeeming Jocasta: Tawfiq al-Hakim's 'Eastern,' 'Arab' reception of Sophocles' *Oedipus Tyrannus*," *Classical Receptions Journal* 11, no. 1 (2019): 100–16.

71. Bowlby, *Freudian Mythologies*, 174.

72. In his exploration of the "Jocasta complex" and of what he calls "Jocasta mothering," Matthew Besdine answers a possible objection to his own, admittedly curious, arguments about mothering, genius, and homosexuality (do note that Merope appears, if fleetingly, under her other name). "To the possible objection that Jocasta did not rear her son, it must be remembered that Queen Periboea of Corinth, hungering for children, adopted Oedipus. He was her only son and heir to the throne. The very causes of Jocasta mothering were present in the royal family of Corinth." Matthew Besdine, "The Jocasta Complex: Mothering and Genius, Part I," *Psychoanalytic Review* 55, no. 2 (1968): 259–77.

73. Besdine, 270; it goes without saying that Besdine never attends to the fact of dual motherhood.

74. Nicole Loraux, "L'empreinte de Jocaste," in Loraux, *La Grèce hors d'elle et autres textes: Écrits 1973-2003*, Michèle Cohen-Halimi, ed. (Paris: Klincksieck, 2021), 501.

75. Loraux, 500.

76. Loraux, 502; and think of Loraux's *Divided City*.

77. Loraux, 503.

78. Loraux, 507.

79. Loraux, 507.

3. THE SOVEREIGNTY OF MOTHERS

1. The shrinking, or *contraction*, of distance, indeed, the *contact* that asymptotically allows the *contraction* of a disease (like love, in earlier times), sustains the wordplay I cite here. It should alter the all-too easily presumed voluntaristic nature of the *contract* (the moment of exchange) as well as its temporality, opening it to the indefinite perdurance of a contact that includes interdependency. Mothers and time. Insisting on the "horizontal sphere of exchange" that ethics is or should be, Willett proposes "cultivating the social eroticism that can find its roots in the relationship between nurturers and child." Cynthia Willett, *Maternal Ethics and Other Slave Moralities* (New York: Routledge, 1995), 8. In her argument, ethics expands into aesthetics and, more precisely, toward "the kinesthetics (touches, scents, sounds) of an originary social bond" (16). What Willett calls "the social dance of early childhood" (16) speaks to the "configuration of maternal space as an organic site of nourishment, tactile attachment, and fluid boundaries" (23). Thus "rhythms, mood changes, and energy levels . . . are transferred between infant and caregiver" (26). This "transferral of kinetic rhythms" (27), this "tactile sociality" (31), which Willett grounds in Luce Irigaray's rewriting of the social contract by way of touch, occurs prior to any market logic, sustaining it and much else, there where there would be "an exchange of feelings . . . a tactile attunement" (41), a "social exchange" (45), "a system regulating exchanges" (46), a contact as contract, a contract as contact.

2. The "form of the contract," upon which Deleuze insists (and which he opposes to institution and law, if not explicitly to sovereignty), disturbingly evokes "the idea of the jurists of antiquity that slavery itself is based on a contract." Gilles Deleuze, "Coldness and Cruelty," trans. Jean McNeil, in *Masochism* (New York: Zone, 1991), 75. Slavery, yes, which can hardly be disentangled from the very notion of a contract. Yet, that same contract demands, and necessarily so, something that is, in our own world of modern "freedom," increasingly unimaginable, namely the notion whereby is retained "a degree of reciprocity of duties, a time limit, a preservation of inalienable rights (the right of work or the subject's honor)."

3. Sara Ruddick writes that "science, like any other kind of thinking, presupposes communities of participants, shared goals, and an agreement that some methods of reaching goals are appropriate while others are

not." Sara Ruddick, *Maternal Thinking: Toward a Politics of Peace* (Boston: Beacon, 1995), 15. Quite a parallel can be made with motherhood, which is not quite the same as to say that, "as diverse as any other humans" as mothers are, they are "equally shaped by the social milieu in which they work" (17). Mothers, like scientists, I suppose, partake of the shaping as well. They respond, reiterate and reinscribe collectives, goals, and methods, and more.

4. Consider the truism offered by Winnicott as he addresses mothers: "You are founding the health of a person who will be a member of our society." Donald Winnicott, *The Child, the Family and the Outside World* (Cambridge, Mass: Perseus, 1987), 26. The person, any person, will definitely be a (hopefully good enough) member of society, and not only by virtue of health, "the foundations of health . . . laid down by the ordinary mother" or mothers (44). Indeed, "the only true basis for a relation of a child to mother and father, to other children, and eventually to society, is the first successful relationship between the mother and baby, between two people" (34). Or again, "the mother's body provides a 'blue-print' for all types of experiences in which instinct is involved" (54). And here too, not only instinct.

5. In his study of "Capital in the Twenty-First Century," Thomas Piketty underscores the necessity of a transgenerational approach that considers together "the history of demographic and economic growth." Thomas Piketty, *Capital in the Twenty-First Century,* trans. Arthur Goldhammer (Cambridge, Mass.: Belknap Press of Harvard University Press, 2014), 84. After all, "capital accumulation is a long-term process extending over several generations" (372). Money was always yet another means of reproduction, of "intergenerational reproduction" (484). So knew Aristotle, who, Piketty recalls, "observed that the word 'interest' in Greek (*tocos*) means 'child.' In his view, money ought not to 'give birth' to more money" (530); and see, for a different perspective on transgenerational accumulations, Robert Meister, *Justice Is an Option: A Democratic Theory of Finance for the Twenty-First Century* (Chicago: University of Chicago Press, 2021); Meister quotes Michel Aglietta, who avers that money is "the intergenerational bond that guarantees the immortality of society" (4).

6. Charles Mills is hardly alone in identifying the social—and the racial—contract as an origin story, an account of foundations. Charles W. Mills, *The Racial Contract* (Ithaca: Cornell University Press, 1997). And it is, of course, but where to begin? The chicken or the egg? With fully grown

adult men shaking on it? With a heterosexual couple going at it? Or with the sovereign subject endowed with freedom? And when did these begin? The arbitrariness of any beginning, and infinite regress, being obvious, I am attending to what seems to me a neglected, and no less fictitious, beginning—mothers—and proposing that the maternal contract frames and folds the question of time, and of signatories, otherwise. It otherwise constitutes the political.

7. For Virginia Held, "the practice of mothering," which involves mostly, but not only, women, justifies the use of "mothering person" rather than "mother." Virginia Held, "Non-contractual Society: A Feminist View," *Canadian Journal of Philosophy* 13 (1987): 116. I do not disagree but, for paleonymic and political reasons, I have preferred *mother*, as verb and (plural) noun; and see Eva Feder Kittay's for whom the dependency relationship is "ubiquitous" and "fundamental" to human society. Eva Feder Kittay, *Love's Labor: Essays on Women, Equality and Dependency* (New York: Routledge, 2020), 30. It is also *necessary* since "it is equally clear that no society will continue beyond one generation if there are not persons who care for the young" (33). Or the old. The paradigmatic dependency workers are, obviously, mothers. What Kittay calls *Doulia*—mother and slave, the maternal contract—is therefore not a mere principle, nor does it emerge from dependency as "a central feature of social organization" (128). It is also more than "a basis for welfare" (140). It is a necessary condition for any collective to perdure in time.

8. Ifi Amadiume, *Reinventing Africa: Matriarchy, Religion and Culture* (London: Zed, 1997), 18; Erella Shadmi, ed., *The Legacy of Mothers: Matriarchies and the Gift Economy as Post-Capitalist Alternatives* (Toronto: Inanna, 2021); and Heide Goettner-Abendroth, *Matriarchal Societies: Studies on Indigenous Cultures Across the Globe* (New York: Peter Lang, 2012).

9. Elva F. Orozco Mendoza, "Responsibility Without Sovereignty: Inaugurating a Maternal Contract to Find the Mexican 'Disappeared' Through Protest and Social Media," in Olivia Guntarik and Victoria Grieve-Williams, eds., *From Sit-ins to #revolutions: Media and the Changing Nature of Protests* (New York: Bloomsbury, 2020), 263.

10. Orozco Mendoza, 270.

11. Orozco Mendoza, 272.

12. The literature about transgenerational trauma has been growing, as has the concern with intergenerational justice, which refers mostly to relations between generations (the latter a reinvented, and mightily abridged,

formation under digital capitalism). The duration, the reproduction of the collective in time, and transgenerationally, seems essential to recognize beyond the uncertain boundaries of family, which, with few exceptions (i.e., trauma), remains the dominant context for "a transgenerational theory" as it was formulated early on by Stuart Lieberman. Stuart Lieberman, "A Transgenerational Theory," *Journal of Family Therapy* 1 (1979): 347–60.

13. Commenting on the work of Naomi Gerstel, Eva Feder Kittay explains of a particular mother that "since her mother gave care to her mother, her mother is now owed care. And as the care her mother's mother received was meted out by the daughter, so that daughter now deserves care from her own daughter" (*Love's Labor*, 72). An allegory of motherhood, of the maternal contract. Kittay knows that "society is an association that persists through generations" (116), yet she invokes a *moral* and "social responsibility" that remain contingent, and she therefore insists on the obligation of care, on the nonfungible moral dimension of such relations of interdependency, rather than on the necessity of reproduction. "A society cannot be well-ordered" without principles of care and responsibility, that is true, but I argue, more simply, that a society cannot maintain itself over time at all without mothers and mothering, without a maternal contract. I argue, in other words, for the political as maternal.

14. After Laura Briggs, I suppose I have been asking not *How All Politics Became Reproductive Politics* but rather how reproduction could ever have been understood as "merely" sexual or indeed economic. Laura Briggs, *How All Politics Became Reproductive Politics from Welfare Reform to Foreclosure to Trump* (Berkeley: University of California Press, 2017). How did mothers become mere (ah but free and independent, if not sovereign) individuals? How did anyone? *Born* free, yes? But without mothers?

15. Mills, *The Racial Contract*, 37. As Deleuze suggests, it might well be the case that "to imagine that a contract or quasi contract is at the origin of society is to invoke conditions which are necessarily invalidated as soon as the law comes into being" (Deleuze, "Coldness and Cruelty," 92). But what law? Further on, Deleuze contemplates the possibility for the law to "become essentially maternal, leading into those regions of the unconscious where the three images of the mother hold supreme sway" (102).

16. Zakiyyah Iman Jackson, *Becoming Human: Matter and Meaning in an Antiblack World* (New York: New York University Press, 2020),143; a few pages before, Jackson pointed to another crucial opposition to be undone: "The

primitive community," she writes, "has long been imagined as the obverse of the *sovereign individual,* held to be the bedrock of a Western civilization that has left behind the prehistoric primitive mind and primal horde," and mother, one might add (139).

17.   Walter Benjamin, "The Task of the Translator," trans. Harry Zohn, in Benjamin, *Selected Writings, Volume 1,* Marcus Bullock and Michael W. Jennings, eds. (Cambridge, Mass.: Belknap Press of Harvard University Press, 1996), 253–63; and see Gil Anidjar, *Blood: A Critique of Christianity* (New York: Columbia University Press, 2014), 9–11.

18.   Penelope Deutscher refers a number of times to the "sovereign-like power over human life" attributed (but apparently not claimed) by women. Penelope Deutscher, *Foucault's Futures: A Critique of Reproductive Reason* (New York: Columbia University Press, 2017), 4. Deutscher does describe the mother as "a remnant of a sovereign mode" (90), but then settles on a more skeptical phrasing whereby "a pseudosovereign capacity to harm embryos, children, and futures" is again "attributed" to women (36, 104, 120, 127)—but why pseudosovereignty? Is this capacity, this power, only *attributed* to mothers? There are reasons here to reflect on abortion and on infanticide beyond a narrowly defined "politics of reproduction," indeed, within the confines of what Deutscher rightly insists on engaging together, namely, biopolitics. By arguing for sovereignty, I do not mean to negate or diminish "the powerlessness of mothers," which Sara Ruddick, for instance, underscores (Ruddick, *Maternal Thinking,* 35). I merely want to indicate that the power of mothers, their capacity to preserve or kill, is not reducible to something a child imagines ("to a child, a mother is huge," writes Ruddick [34]). Nor is maternal powerlessness limited to experiences of failure or of social impotence. As Ruddick also writes, "Real maternal power is not a stable quantity" (36).

19.   Leïla Slimani, *Lullaby,* trans. Sam Taylor (London: Faber & Faber, 2018), a fantastic book, and not only for the conversions and reversals it performs, to be read together with Alice Diop's film, *Saint Omer.*

20.   Roberto Esposito, *Immunitas: The Protection and Negation of Life,* trans. Zakiya Hanafi (Cambridge: Polity, 2011), 170; and see Mark C. Taylor, *Nots* (Chicago: University of Chicago Press, 1993), 251–52.

21.   It is as Nancy Hirschmann says, a *power,* and it is "because it is a power that men are compelled to conquer women." Nancy J. Hirschmann, *Gender, Class, and Freedom in Modern Political Theory* (Princeton: Princeton University Press, 2008), 54.

22. Simone de Beauvoir, *The Second Sex,* trans. Constance Borde and Sheila Malovany-Chevalier (New York: Vintage, 2011), 552; Silvia Federici, *Caliban and the Witch: Women, the Body and Primitive Accumulation* (New York: Autonomedia, 2004), 88–89. The enmity between mother and child, between child and mother is not merely of an "emotional" nature. It is about power, about a contest of powers, and most specifically, a contest between sovereignty and slavery. I shall not rehearse here Carl Schmitt's theories regarding sovereignty and enmity. Suffice it to say that the decision over the exception, the power of miracles, or the existential struggle with an enemy that interrogates one's very existence, "the real possibility of physical killing"—these gain, in the maternal context that is mine here, renewed pertinence. Carl Schmitt, *The Concept of the Political,* trans. George Schwab (Chicago: University of Chicago Press, 2007), 33.

23. Cheryl L. Meyer and Michelle Oberman, with Kelly White, Michelle Rone, Priya Batra, and Tara C. Proano, *Mothers Who Kill Their Children: Understanding the Acts of Moms from Susan Smith to the 'Prom Mom'"* (New York: New York University Press, 2001), but the literature on infanticide is quite vast, as I shall go on to reiterate, even if it remains confined to the criminal or the psychological, at times the cultural (most studies showing themselves highly respectful of national boundaries, in fact).

24. Gil Anidjar, "That Great Mother of Danger," *Critical Times* 6, no. 2 (August 2023): 257–70.

25. Gil Anidjar, *Qu'appelle-t-on destruction? Heidegger, Derrida* (Montréal: Presses de l'université de Montréal, 2017).

26. *Three-Text Edition of Thomas Hobbes' Political Theory: The Elements of Law, De Cive and Leviathan* (Cambridge: Cambridge University Press, 2017), Deborah Baumgold, ed.: *The Elements of Law,* ch. 23.

27. *Three-Text Edition of Thomas Hobbes' Political Theory, De Cive,* ch. 9, 287–88.

28. Carol Pateman, *The Sexual Contract* (Stanford: Stanford University Press, 1988), 44; Pateman says nothing more about this contract, by which "the infant" (why not "the child?") agrees that "being grown to full age he become not her enemy," as Hobbes puts it. The contract puts an end to enmity, not just between mothers and infants, but between mothers and children (adult children?) over time. Pateman is explicit that she does not write about "women as mothers" (209), yet she surprisingly cuts the Gordian knot on the chicken and the egg, that is, on the origins of the social contract and of the family. For her, "the origin of the family" is found "in the relation between husband and wife. The fact that men and women

enter into a marriage contract—an 'original' contract that constitutes marriage and the family—and are husbands and wives *before* they are fathers and mothers is forgotten" (27); so why is "original" in scare quotes? Does saying that one "starts" a family make it a beginning? A true origin? If the social contract is a fiction, a fiction of origins, why does it have to find its sole origin in fully-formed adults rather than in the bond that binds, over time, mother and child?

29. *Three-Text Edition of Thomas Hobbes' Political Theory*, De Cive, ch. 9, 287.

30. Rosamond Scott, *Rights, Duties and the Body: Law and Ethics of the Maternal-Fetal Conflict* (Portland: Hart, 2002).

31. *Three-Text Edition of Thomas Hobbes' Political Theory*, 287; the difference between Hobbes and Locke could not be more significant on this point. As Jeremy Waldron explains, Locke is quite radical in recognizing and advocating the equality of the parents, mother and father, but he does so by denying any political relevance to parenting ("Parental power may not be political power. Locke is adamant about that"), let alone to mothering. Jeremy Waldron, " 'The Mother Too Hath Her Title'—John Locke on Motherhood and Equality," Public Law and Legal Theory Research Paper Series, New York University School of Law, Working Paper 10–74 (October 2010), 23. Hobbes, by contrast, grants mothers an originary sovereignty and requires us, therefore, to rethink the political out of the maternal.

32. Pateman, *The Sexual Contract*; Adriana Cavarero, *Horrorism: Naming Contemporary Violence*, trans. William McCuaig (New York: Columbia University Press, 2010); Hirschmann, *Gender, Class, and Freedom in Modern Political Theory*; and see Nancy Hirschmann and Joanne H. Wright, eds., *Feminist Interpretations of Thomas Hobbes* (University Park: Pennsylvania State University Press, 2012).

33. Thomas Hobbes, *On the Citizen*, Richard Tuck, ed. (Cambridge: Cambridge University Press, 1998), 102; there, Hobbes is elaborating on his notion of dominion, on master and slave; and recall that, as Joan Cocks explains, Hobbes's "first premise is the principle of the natural liberty of every individual to use his own power as he chooses to preserve himself, with a natural right to everything that he sees as a means to that end." Joan Cocks, *On Sovereignty and Other Political Delusions* (London: Bloomsbury, 2014), 32. There would thus be a premise (the mother) before the "first premise," a sovereignty that, as it were, precedes liberty.

34. Walter Benjamin, *Berlin Childhood Around 1900,* trans. Howard Eiland (Cambridge, Mass.: Belknap Press of Harvard University Press, 2006), 77 and 112; and his "Critique of Violence," trans. Edmund Jephcott, in Walter Benjamin *Selected Writings*, Markus Bullock and Michael W. Jennings, eds. (Cambridge, Mass.: Belknap Press of Harvard University Press, 1996), 236–52; Peter Fenves, almost alone among critics in remarking Niobe's maternality, writes that mythical violence "attacks in a differential manner—mothers first." Peter Fenves, " 'Out of the Order of Number': Benjamin and Irigaray Toward a Politics of Pure Means," *Diacritics* 28, no. 1 (Spring 1998): 52.

35. Su Fang Ng, "Hobbes and the Bestial Body of Sovereignty," in Hirschmann and Wright, *Feminist Interpretations of Thomas Hobbes*, 96; I see no reason to reduce "the sovereign space of maternal power" to the subjective "choice" of abortion as Adriana Cavarero does. Cavarero, *In Spite of Plato: A Feminist Rewriting of Ancient Philosophy,* trans. Serena Anderlini-D'Onofrio and Áine O'Healy (New York: Routledge, 1995), 75.

36. Nancy A. Stanlick, "Lords and Mothers: Silent Subjects in Hobbes's Political Theory," in Patrick Hayden and Tom Lansford, eds., *Politics and Ethics* (New York: Nova Science, 2002), 143; substituting "mothers" for Stanlick's "women." And see Petra Bueskens, who agrees that, in Hobbes, "motherhood functions as the first 'contract' since the infant must 'consent' to be governed by the mother or else die. In effect, mother right is the foundation of the state, even though it is traded away very early." Petra Bueskens, *Modern Motherhood and Women's Dual Identities: Rewriting the Sexual Contract* (New York: Routledge, 2018), 91n3. Bueskens adheres to the sovereignty of women and to the mother as foundation.

37. In *Sovereignty and Its Other: Toward the Dejustification of Violence* (New York: Fordham University Press, 2013), Dimitris Vardoulakis explores the indissociable and conflictual link between sovereignty and democracy. As Plato's *Laws* have it, of which Vardoulakis reminded me, these would constitute two mothers, two regimes, two constitutions (monarchy and democracy, sovereignty and contract) that are and must be woven together. For the collective to perdure, that is.

38. I already mentioned that the very phrase "maternal sovereignty" is a rarity. In her exploration of the problem of domination, Jessica Benjamin, for instance, grants sovereignty to the baby, but never to the mother. John Bowlby does write of the mother or mother-figure that she "becomes so central a figure in the infant's life" when "in healthy development it is

towards her that each of the several responses becomes directed, much as each of the subjects of the realm comes to direct his loyalty towards the Queen; and it is in relation to the mother that the several responses become integrated into the complex behaviour which I have termed 'attachment behaviour,' much as it is in relation to the Sovereign that the components of our constitution become integrated into a working whole. We may extend the analogy. It is in the nature of our constitution, as of all others, that sovereignty is vested in a single person." John Bowlby, "The Nature of the Child's Tie to His Mother," *International Journal of Psycho-Analysis* 39 (1958): 369–70.

39. Deutscher writes that "reproduction compresses multiple states of revocability" (Deutscher, *Foucault's Futures*, 140); incidentally, Deutscher acknowledges that "abortion controversies have been contexts in which women may find themselves associated with agencies of death (fetal, individual, collective, population, and future)," but for Deutscher "these associations and their conjoined revocability" must be understood as only "one of the senses of thanatopoliticized reproduction" (143). I argue that these associations, which are not merely "attributed," demand a more sustained reflection on maternal sovereignty, on the maternal contract.

40. Donald Winnicott, "The Use of an Object and Relating Through Identifications," in Donald Winnicott, *Playing and Reality* (New York: Routledge, 2005), 115–27; Thomas H. Ogden, "Destruction Reconceived: On Winnicott's 'The Use of an Object and Relating Through Identifications,'" *International Journal of Psychoanalysis* 97, no. 5 (2016): 1243–62.

41. Amber Jacobs, *On Matricide: Myth, Psychoanalysis, and the Law of the Mother* (New York: Columbia University Press, 2007); and see Joy James, "Madea v. Medea: Agape and the Militarist or Murderous Maternal," in LeRhonda S. Manigualt-Bryant, Tamura A. Lomax, and Carol B. Duncan, eds. *Womanist and Black Feminist Responses to Tyler Perry's Production* (New York: Palgrave MacMillan, 2014), 187–200.

42. Ruth Tsoffar, *Life in Citations: Biblical Narratives and Contemporary Hebrew Culture* (New York: Routledge, 2020), 30; I have only recently discovered Jean-Christophe Attias's beautiful *Moïse fragile* (Paris: Alma, 2015), which devotes an entire chapter to "La femme Moïse"; now the title of the translated book, *A Woman Called Moses: A Prophet for Our Times,* trans. Gregory Elliott (London: Verso, 2020).

43. Caroline Walker Bynum, *Jesus as Mother: Studies in the Spirituality of the High Middle Ages* (Berkeley: University of California Press, 1982).

44. Numbers 11:10–15 (*JPS* translation); Lisa Guenther, *The Gift of the Other: Levinas and the Politics of Reproduction* (Albany: State University of New York Press, 2006), 129–40; Jean-Christophe Attias, who insists that Moses was (also) a *woman* comments "Everything is in the masculine, obviously, but the role that is so burdensome to Moses, which God has forced on him, and which he feels incapable of performing, manifestly possesses all the attributes of a maternal role" (Attias, *A Woman Called Moses,* 67).

45. Cynthia Chapman finds "the entire female-focused process of child formation presented in this text, where Moses conceives, gives birth, carries, and breastfeeds a rebellious people who are referred to metaphorically as a 'suckling'" or *yōnēq.* Cynthia R. Chapman, *The House of the Mother: The Social Roles of Maternal Kin in Biblical Hebrew Narrative and Poetry* (New Haven: Yale University Press, 2016), 145.

46. The Hebrew term is *omen,* the masculine of *omenet,* which we encountered earlier. It is also the term translated as "nursing fathers" and, more precisely, "your nursing fathers, *omanayikh*" in Isaiah 49:23, quoted earlier as well; and see Deena Aranoff, "The Biblical Root *'mn*: Retrieval of a Term and Its Household Context," in Marjorie Lehman, Jane L. Kanarek, and Simon J. Bronner, eds., *Mothers in the Jewish Cultural Imagination* (Liverpool: Litman Library of Jewish Civilization and Liverpool University Press, 2017), 327–41.

47. Michel Foucault, *Security, Territory, Population: Lectures at the Collège de France 1977-78,* trans. Graham Burchell (New York: Palgrave Macmillan, 2009), 126–30; as Joëlle Marelli points out to me, Foucault does not mention the sacrifice—the slaughter—of the sheep at some altar or other. Nor does he concern himself with the beneficiary of the pastoral arrangement (shepherds rarely work for their own benefit, nor really for the sheep's).

48. Mara Benjamin understands the conversation between Moses and God as the argument of "two caregivers over the recalcitrance of their child." Mara H. Benjamin, *The Obligated Self: Maternal Subjectivity and Jewish Thought* (Bloomington: Indiana University Press, 2018), 66; and see Don C. Benjamin, "Israel's God: Mother and Midwife," *Biblical Theology Bulletin* 19, no. 4 (November 1989): 114–58.

49. "To deprive a people of the man whom they take pride in as the greatest of their sons is not a thing to be gladly or carelessly undertaken, least of all by someone who is himself one of them." Sigmund Freud, *Moses and Monotheism,* in *The Standard Edition of the Complete Psychological Works,* James Strachey, ed. (London: Hogarth and Institute of Psycho-Analysis, 1961),

23:7; I have attended to this and other aspects of Freud's *Moses* in *Blood,* 235–55.

50. Numbers 11:16–17.

51. Guenther, *The Gift of the Other,* 136; Mara Benjamin discerns here a "portrayal of God's maternal subjectivity" (Benjamin, *The Obligated Self,* 66).

52. Guenther, *The Gift of the Other,* 138.

53. Guenther, 139.

54. There are plenty of excellent reasons why Simone de Beauvoir began her chapter on motherhood with a discussion of abortion, just as there are for Adrienne Rich to devote her final chapter to violence and infanticide in *Of Woman Born.*

55. Jacques Derrida and Elisabeth Roudinesco, *For What Tomorrow . . . a Dialogue,* trans. Jeff Fort (Stanford: Stanford University Press, 2004, 140); Derrida asks why it is that those who claim to be on the side of life, and therefore against abortion, are the most ardent partisans of the death penalty. He might have added, as Simone de Beauvoir did, that those "men who most respect embryonic life are the same ones who do not hesitate to send adults to death in war . . . [just as] the Church authorizes the killing of adult men in war, or when it is a question of the death penalty; but it stands on intransigent humanitarianism for the fetus" (Beauvoir, *The Second Sex,* 525).

56. Mills, *The Racial Contract,* 4; Kathleen Davis has powerfully demonstrated the link between sovereignty and time, between sovereignty and history. Kathleen Davis, *Periodization and Sovereignty: How Ideas of Feudalism and Secularization Govern the Politics of Time* (Philadelphia: University of Pennsylvania Press, 2008). What Davis calls "the cut of periodization" functions as a "disappearing trick" (18) whereby the complex history of an emerging free and sovereign subject (individual or collective) would have been preceded by darker antecedents, darker continents. In fact, periodization redistributes across the medieval/modern divide the very terms upon which theories of sovereignty are articulated, "the subjected and the sovereign, the enslaved and the free" (8). My own argument on sovereignty and slavery obviously aligns with Davis who herself attends to the role and the significance of slavery and explains that "professional jurists theorized sovereignty, subjection, and a social contract on the basis of the feudal relation of lord and vassal" before "legal historians such as Jean Bodin advanced arguments for absolutism by retaining this theory of the social contract" (24).

57. Juliet Mitchell, *Fratriarchy: The Sibling Trauma and the Law of the Mother* (New York: Routledge, 2022), 184.

58. See Jacques Derrida, *The Death Penalty* (Chicago: University of Chicago Press, 2017); Eyal Weizman, *The Least of All Possible Evils: Humanitarian Violence from Arendt to Gaza* (London: Verso, 2011).

59. Soran Reader, "Abortion, Killing, and Maternal Moral Authority," *Hypatia* 23, no. 1 (January–March 2008): 132–49; and see Mary Poovey, "The Abortion Question and the Death of Man," in Judith Butler and Joan Scott, eds., *Feminists Theorize the Political* (New York: Routledge, 1992), 239–56; but there are historical and cultural differences, of course, see, e.g., Nora E. Jaffary, "Reconceiving Motherhood: Infanticide and Abortion in Colonial Mexico," *Journal of Family History* 37, no. 1 (2012): 3–22.

60. Jacqueline Rose, *Mothers* (New York: Farrar, Straus & Giroux, 2018), 94; as Rose further explains, "unless the world is kept in its shape by the mother, there can be no imaginative freedom. Unless there is a mother, there can be no world" (173); commenting on Ferrante's vision, Rose adds that "a mother's body and the public world all around her are indissolubly linked" (175). What, then, what indeed, "is a mother meant to do in such a world?" (176).

61. Another vast body of literature that does not send us to a distant (and exclusively Nazi) past; see, e.g., Alexandra Minna Stern, *Eugenic Nation: Faults and Frontiers of Better Breeding in Modern America* (Berkeley: University of California Press, 2005), which includes an important discussion of the U.S. Border Patrol.

62. Yan Thomas, *La mort du père: Sur le crime de parricide à Rome* (Paris: Albin Michel, 2017), where Thomas explains the absolute power of life and death held by the father over his children. It is that power and status, the dominance and unquestioned ownership of the father, which explains why parricide (and not infanticide) was the gravest of crimes. In a chapter on the mother's belly (*venter*), Thomas also ponders the surprising fact that abortion never became a legal or criminal matter (111–12).

63. Anne Dufourmantelle, *La sauvagerie maternelle* (Paris: Calmann-Lévy, 2001), 20.

64. In a paper written for a seminar I taught on "Mothers," the journalist Amel Brahmi described those French legislators who seek to enforce *laïcité* on veil-wearing mothers (and not only on teachers and students or employees of the state). Some of those legislators "suggested turning mothers into state agents by redefining the status of parent volunteers who could

be defined as 'all people participating in the public service of education' or 'occasional collaborators to the public service.' One generous elected official offered to pay the mothers so they'll be officially working for the city as civil servants." Only the prohibitive cost put an end to that intriguing idea. Amel Brahmi, unpublished paper, Columbia University, Spring 2022. The reasoning of that official is admittedly terrible, but it does include a recognition of mothers as agents of the collective.

65. On that protracted series of chapters in human, all-too human history, I have learned much from Alice Diop's film, *Saint Omer* (2022) and from Nancy Scheper-Hughes, *Death Without Weeping: The Violence of Everyday Life in Brazil* (Berkeley: University of California Press, 1992), but see also William Langer, "Infanticide: A Historical Survey," *History of Childhood Quarterly* 1, no. 3 (Winter 1974): 353–65 and "Further Notes on the History of Infanticide," *History of Childhood Quarterly* 2, no. 1 (Summer 1974): 129–34. Like the literature on "violence," the coverage is obviously quite vast, and reaches from the primatological, anthropological, cultural, and/or national to a marked preference for the psychological and the criminal. It is made vaster by the recognition that infanticide has served the functions we now associate with contraception and with abortion, not to mention eugenic policies (see the following note).

66. "We come mighty close [to eugenic thinking and practices] when we once again let scientists and physicians make judgments about who should and who should not inhabit the world and applaud them when they develop the technologies that let us implement such judgments," writes Ruth Hubbard in "Abortion and Disability: Who Should and Should Not Inhabit the World," in Lennard J. Davis, ed., *The Disability Studies Reader*, 4th ed. (New York: Routledge, 2013), 84; Hubbard goes on to say that "a woman must have the right to terminate a pregnancy, whatever her reasons, but she must also feel empowered not to terminate it, confident that the society will do what it can to enable her and her child to live fulfilling lives," confident that the society will mother her as a mother (85).

67. Virginie Despentes, *King Kong Theory,* trans. Stéphanie Benson (New York: Feminist Press at the City University of New York, 2010), 23; and compare Kittler, who writes that "in the Mother the state found its Other," which leads, he says, to placing "the function of Motherhood above all political considerations," Friedrich Kittler, *Discourse Networks 1800/1900*, trans. Michael Metteer and Chris Cullens (Stanford: Stanford University Press, 1990), 58. For Kittler, there are thus "two authorities, state and Mother,"

the latter remaining unwritten in the former's discursive network (66). Silvia Federici gives a powerful account of the long and harsh history Kittler attends to (Federici, *Caliban and the Witch*).

68. Lee Edelman, in *No Future: Queer Theory and the Death Drive* (Durham: Duke University Press, 2004); Eva Feder Kittay, who also reminds us of the ill, the elderly, and the disabled, formulates the question (albeit in the singular) as "Who is to care for the caregiver?" (Kittay, *Love's Labor*, 70), and compare Virginia Held, who was asked and herself asks, "who are the mothers and who are the children?" (Held, "Non-contractual Society," 136).

69. Ruddick, *Maternal Thinking*, 47; Ruddick is clear on the need for communities to "support the work of mothering and the well-being of children with free and effective medical services, day-care centers, flexible working hours, and pervasive respect for maternal work" (45), though what she describes sets not only quite low an expectation, it strangely confines "maternal work" to an all-too limited realm.

70. "The Father, the Law, the Animal, etc., the sovereign and the beast—should one not recognize here basically one and the same thing? Or, rather, indissociable figures of the same Thing? One could add the Mother, and it probably would change nothing." Jacques Derrida, *The Beast and the Sovereign*, vol. 1, trans. Geoffrey Bennington (Chicago: University of Chicago Press, 2009), 127. Much hangs on the word *probably*, of course.

71. Toni Morrison, *Beloved: A Novel* (New York: Vintage, 2004), 165.

72. "Morrison explores dimensions of sovereign power that often go undetected and unremarked" (Jackson, *Becoming Human*, 61); for Jackson, it is however Mr. Garner who, in his capacity "to give and bestow, to create and legitimate," is "emblematic" of sovereignty (62). Garner is the last name of the historical figure upon whom Morrison partly drew; see Mark Reinhardt, *Who Speaks for Margaret Garner?* (Minneapolis: University of Minnesota Press, 2010), where the question of sovereignty is demonstrably raised by the sources; and see Nikki Marie Taylor, *Driven Toward Madness: The Fugitive Slave Margaret Garner and Tragedy on the Ohio* (Athens: Ohio University Press, 2016).

73. Carl Schmitt proposed the figure of the *katechon*, the "retainer" who holds off the end of the world, who "holds down the chaos that pushes up from below." Jacob Taubes, *The Political Theology of Paul*, trans. Dana Hollander (Stanford: Stanford University Press, 2004), 103; Schmitt's translator has "restrainer" for *katechon*, described as "the historical power to *restrain* the

appearance of the Antichrist and the end of the present eon; it was a power that withholds." Carl Schmitt, *The Nomos of the Earth in the International Law of the* Jus Public Europaeum, trans. G. L. Ulmen (New York: Telos, 2003), 60. Others might recognize here Jacques Derrida's autoimmunity, in which the one guards and keeps the other, it keeps the other for itself, but also guards itself from the other. If, as I have argued elsewhere, Derrida's thinking turned and returned to the maternal (Anidjar, "Solicitude" in *Derrida Today* 16, no. 1 (2023), 3–19), there should be little surprise in having reached this point.

74. Winnicott underscores that mothers, a.k.a., "the environment" ("the mother is the environment and the provider of the ordinary physical necessities of security, warmth, and freedom from the unpredictable" (Winnicott, *The Child, the Family and the Outside World*, 52), are "a preventer rather than a curer" (78). Mothers must "introduce the world in small doses, so that the baby is not confused" (27, 69ff.). Life being "just a series of terrifically intense experiences" (70), the world—the real—must be softened, mediated, or indeed, kept at bay. Thus, "a great deal depends on the way the world is presented to the infant and to the growing child" (74).

CODA

1. Paul Rabinow, *French Modern: Norms and Forms of the Social Environment* (Cambridge, Mass.: MIT Press, 1989), 306; and see, for a rich and nuanced account, Emily Gottreich, *Jewish Morocco: A History from Pre-Islamic to Postcolonial Times* (London: I. B. Tauris, 2020).

2. Abdelmalek Sayad, *The Suffering of the Immigrant,* trans. David Macey (Cambridge: Polity, 2004).

3. Laura Esquivel, *Like Water for Chocolate*, trans. Carol Christensen and Thomas Christensen (New York: Doubleday, 1992), 8.

4. Richard A. Lobban Jr., *Cape Verde: Crioulo Colony to Independent Nation* (New York: Routledge, 2018), 55.

5. Amnon Raz-Krakotzkin, *Exil et souveraineté: Judaïsme, sionisme et pensée binationale,* trans. Catherine Neuve-Église (Paris: La Fabrique, 2007).

6. Houria Bouteldja, *Whites, Jews, and Us: Toward a Politics of Revolutionary Love,* trans. Rachel Valinsky (South Pasadena, Calif.: Semiotext(e), 2018), 27.

7. To reiterate, "Mothers in the home are expected to manage more or less on their own—one of feminism's loudest, most persistent and fairest

complaints—but the one thing a mother cannot possibly manage by herself is mothering" (Rose, *Mothers*, 32).

8. Ella Shohat, 'Coming to America:' Reflections on Hair and Memory Loss" in *On the Arab-Jew, Palestine, and Other Displacements: Selected Writings* (London: Pluto Press, 2017), 353; Shohat locates the split in time and place, between Iraq and Israel, between photographs and broken body.

9. Sara Ruddick, *Maternal Thinking*, 18.

10. Deleuze, "Coldness and Cruelty," 63.

11. Muraro, *The Symbolic Order of the Mother*, 65.

12. Samir Ben-Layashi and Bruce Maddy-Weitzman, "Myth, History, and Realpolitik: Morocco and its Jewish Community," *Journal of Modern Jewish Studies* 9:1 (2010) 89–106; the authors describe the sense of cultural superiority of Andalusian refugees, both Muslims and Jews, over time.

13. Muraro, *The Symbolic Order of the Mother*, 6.

14. "With me it was always the same thing. Nothing." Emile Ajar, *Momo (Life Before Us)*, trans. Ralph Manheim (Garden City, N.J.: Doubleday, 1978), 25.

15. Stefania Pandolfo, *Knot of the Soul: Madness, Psychoanalysis, Islam* (Chicago: University of Chicago Press, 2018).

16. Albert Swissa, the Moroccan Israeli writer, recently offered his moving commentary on Hagar, telling of the Arab or Berber, Muslim servant or savior, the mother, that marked his childhood and his father's childhood; Swissa recalls Hagar (and Ishmael) to depict the Moroccan immigration to Israel as a "Black" maternal presence, with dependence and denial defining the Zionist state in its relation to "Ishmaelites," primarily to Palestine. Albert Swissa, "Bound Together: My Longings for Ishmael," trans. Gil Anidjar at themarkaz.org/bound-together-my-longings-for-ishmael/.

17. Amnon Raz-Krakotzkin, "Zion: Between Redemption of the Shekhinah and the Unraveling of Hagar," *Hakivun Mizrakh [East-Word]: A Literary-Cultural Review* 17 (2017): 78, (a special issue on Yosef-Joseph Dadoune, in collaboration with the Petach Tikva Museum of Art).

18. "These are my ancestors, these are my people," wrote James, "they are yours too if you want them." C. L. R. James, "The Making of the Caribbean People," in *Spheres of Existence: Selected Writings* (London: Allison and Busby, 1980), p. 187, and see Joëlle Marelli, "Revolutionary Love in Dark Times (review of Bouteldja, *Whites, Jews and Us*)" at www.boundary2.org/2018/11/revolutionaryloveindarktimes/.

19. Ernst H. Kantorowicz, "Pro Patria Mori in Medieval Political Thought," *American Historical Review* 56, no. 3 (April 1951): 472–92.

20. Anna Apostolidou, *Queering the Motherland: Male Same-Sex Desire and the Greek Nation* (Beau Bassin, Mauritius: LAP Lambert Academic, 2018).

21. Howard Eilberg-Schwartz, *God's Phallus and Other Problems for Men and Monotheism* (Boston: Beacon, 1994); Amnon Raz-Krakotzkin, *Mishna Consciousness, Biblical Consciousness: Safed and Zionist Culture* [in Hebrew] (Tel-Aviv: Van Leer Institute Press/Hakibbutz Hameuchad, 2022).

22. See David Carroll, *Albert Camus the Algerian: Colonialism, Terrorism, Justice* (New York: Columbia University Press, 2007), especially 97–105.

23. Anton Shammas, *Arabesques*, trans. Vivian Eden (New York: New York Review Books, 2023), 92.

24. 1 Kings 3:17–18.

25. Bertolt Brecht, *The Caucasian Chalk Circle*, trans. Eric Bentley (Minneapolis: University of Minnesota Press, 1999).

26. 2 Kings 6:24–33; in this story, the king simply tears his clothes in mournful desperation. My reference to a totemic meal is meant to suggest a recasting of Freud's *Totem and Taboo*. A band of mothers.

27. Julie Livingstone, *Self-Devouring Growth: A Planetary Parable As Told From Southern Africa* (Durham: Duke University Press, 2019).

28. Sigmund Freud, *Totem and Taboo*, trans. James Strachey in *The Standard Edition of the Complete Psychological Works*, James Strachey, ed. (London: Hogarth and Institute of Psycho-Analysis, 1961), 13:141.

29. Shammas, *Arabesques*, 255; this sentence is spoken by Michel Abyad, also known as Anton Shammas, a character in Anton Shammas's *Arabesques*, who may or may not have written Shammas's book, or another, under the pseudonym "Anton Shammas." One book or two, but governed and sustained by mothers and grandmothers, and othermothers.

30. "We are, after all, the mother of the child," Palestinians told Amira Hass. This is what "they say, alluding to King Solomon's judgment to explain their readiness to share the country." Amira Hass, *Drinking the Sea at Gaza: Days and Nights in a Land Under Siege*, trans. Elana Wesley and Maxine Kaufman-Lacusta (New York: Metropolitan, 1999), 352.

31. James Baldwin, *The Fire Next Time* (New York: Vintage, 1993), 105; inserting the word *mothers* for Baldwin's "lovers."

32. Shammas, *Arabesques*, 258.

33. Ajar, *Momo (Life Before Us)*, 143; translation altered.

34. Mahmoud Darwish, "Give Birth to Me Again, That I May Know," trans. Abdullah al-Udhari, in *Victims of a Map: A Bilingual Anthology of Arabic Poetry* (London: Saqi, 1995), 21.

INDEX

INDEX

INDEX

Walzer, Michael, 119n33
Ward, Dana, xvii
Warner, Marina, 103n6
Waterman, Barbara, 116n4
Waters, John W., 120n41
Watson, Amanda, 107n39
Watson, Jay, 111n23, 129n25
Weizmann, Eyal, 146n58
Weynbaum, Alys Eve, 127n11
Whitebook, Joel, 130n36, 131n39

Willett, Cynthia, 13, 112n30, 114n46,
  124n80, 126n6, 135n1
Williams, Delores, 35, 36, 120n40,
  123n70
Winnicott, Donald, 13, 46, 110n15,
  113n37, 129n28, 136n4, 143n40,
  149n74

Young, Iris Marion, 104n17, 105n25,
  110n16, 114n46

GPSR Authorized Representative: Easy Access System Europe, Mustamäe tee
50, 10621 Tallinn, Estonia, gpsr.requests@easproject.com

www.ingramcontent.com/pod-product-compliance
Lightning Source LLC
Chambersburg PA
CBHW032138020426
42334CB00016B/1206